Motivate
Your Son

7/13

DATE DUE

Motivate Your Son

Inspire Your Boy To Be Engaged In School, Excited For College, and Energized For Success

DARYL CAPUANO

FOUNDER OF THE LEARNING CONSULTANTS

Student Mastery Publishing
Old Saybrook, CT 06475

Summary: Help for parents seeking to motivate their teenage sons.

ISBN-13: 978-0-9849451-0-8

To Francie, Danny, Kearney, and Katie

Table of Contents

PART III

PART IV

Acknowledgments

This book would not have been completed without Paul Borgese. He is a master of many disciplines. Writing and publishing is simply one of many areas of his brilliance. Paul's books and business ventures are too numerous to enumerate. If you are interested in learning about one of the new masters of the digital age, he is worth a Google search.

Thank you to Dr. Andrew Hahn for providing deep wisdom related to understanding human motivation and personality types. Those who meet Dr. Hahn invariably describe their interactions as life changing. On that count, I am simply one of many. Thank you to Joanne Carter, Kathy Tamborlane, Barbara Stevens, and Carey Bourque from Education Solutions. I am forever grateful for your help in jump-starting my work in this area.

Thank you to my teammates at The Learning Consultants. Each of you has been helpful throughout the years, but I want to particularly thank Dr. Kristina Knobelsdorff for her insightful editorial suggestions. Jean Card, Jesse Brockwell, and Galen Cawley also provided valuable help in furtherance of this book. I am very lucky to have such good friends as colleagues.

Thank you to my parents Len and Treasure Capuano, as well as my brother Duane Capuano and my late grandmother Beatrice Capuano, for their support

Daryl Capuano

through the years. Most importantly, thank you to my wife Francie and my children Danny, Kearney, and Katie for making life such a happy and fun adventure.

PART I

Chapter One

Greatness Awaits

Your son has more opportunity to thrive at a very young age than at any time in history. If things go well in this dynamic age of change, he soon could be living a healthy, balanced lifestyle in a career that he loves. And, yes, he could be very wealthy before he reaches 30.

Even so, if you are standing in a group of three parents of boys, chances are that one of you will have a son who will not be financially independent . . . ever.

Welcome to parenting on the cliff of a beautiful mountain.

The Problem With Boys

I run a company called The Learning Consultants. We serve thousands of clients each year and receive calls for help regarding the full spectrum of educational issues. Many important areas deserve attention, but motivating teen boys is the most pressing need.

I noticed the issue in the early 2000s. Boys seemed to care far less about school than girls. That seemed normal. My high school buddies were motivated by sports and social life, not school. Yet, they mostly blossomed into big successes as they made their way in the world. I assumed that boys in this group would awake from their slumber and begin to thrive as they got older and cared about success. But more calls started coming

1

in from parents of older boys who were not doing well in high school. More distressing, I received an alarming number of urgent calls from parents of young men who were floundering in their transition to college.

I then looked at our client list and services provided. While our company provides educational services in a wide variety of areas for an equal number of boys and girls, the overwhelming majority of calls regarding motivation were for teen boys. The ratio was around 20 to 1. It was a small sample, but I thought I was seeing the beginning of an epidemic of male underachievement.

Sadly, I was right, and worse, I had underestimated the problem.

Data confirmed what I had experienced first-hand: boys and young men are floundering. I will spare you detailed statistics here (see Appendix A if interested), but one is worth memorizing:

At least one of three men between the ages of 22 and 34 is living at home with his parents.[1]

That is an astonishing proportion of young men who have not become financially independent. It also represents a slap in the face warning to parents of boys. Diminished self-esteem and prolonged career struggles are the most present issues confronting these young men. Over time, however, the bigger problem might end up being something unforeseen. I wonder

---

[1] Reread that statistic to get a full measure of its import, with a particular focus on the outer age of 34. Also, note that the economic recession did not contribute to this statistic as it was generated based on an analysis of the 2000 census by the Washington Post's analysis of the 2000 census – well before the Great Recession. I also note that some of those young men living at home are doing so responsibly by holding down a full time job or attending graduate school and that some are doing so because certain cultures prefer that young adults stay with their family until marriage.

how many of these young men will get ever get married and start families.

What is the root cause?

The root cause did not sprout in those who failed to launch in their twenties, but rather in their teen years. Highly successful college graduates do not jettison their ambitions and move back home.

Why then are these twenty-something young men struggling?

For the most part, they floundered in college, either doing poorly or not graduating. Still, this was not the origin of their problems. There was a reason that they had not completed college successfully. While some highly successful high school students perform terribly in college, most do not.

Why then are so many young men performing poorly in college?

In general, these young men did not have great college options and subsequently wound up in either an uninspiring or mismatched college environment for them. In addition, many of these young men did not have the work character to succeed at the college level. Essentially, their college transition did not go well. Yet, while their difficulties were exacerbated during their college years, the initial source of their challenges emerged earlier.

Why didn't these men have optimal college options or the work character to handle college?

In most every case, these young men had sub-par grades in high school and did not develop the proper work character, training, and skills to become competent students. Their poor grades and inadequate preparation are the tangible results of something else.

After working with several thousand students this past decade, I will suggest that 95% of these young men were not properly motivated to do their best when they were teen boys.

We have our root cause for most struggling young men: *lack of motivation during the teen years.*

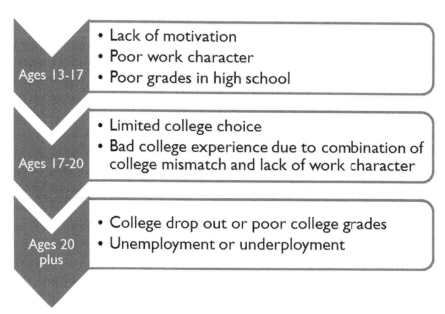

Ages 13-17
- Lack of motivation
- Poor work character
- Poor grades in high school

Ages 17-20
- Limited college choice
- Bad college experience due to combination of college mismatch and lack of work character

Ages 20 plus
- College drop out or poor college grades
- Unemployment or underployment

How Does Your Process Work?

This book is about motivation. But the motivational component of our work is only one part a program that I created called The Student Mastery Program. This program has been the cornerstone for how The Learning Consultants helps students.

The program is designed to teach students how to excel in the job of "student." "Student" is the longest job that most people will ever hold. Yet, there is no training for this job. Motivation is the most critical part of the program, but shifting student psychology is one piece of the whole. There are best practices for student effectiveness that must be instilled after the student is motivated.

On the issue of what it is we actually do, parents naturally want to know how our program works. Not surprisingly, mothers and fathers approach the issue differently. Mothers will discuss their children and our process for helping their children endlessly. I usually have to bring such discussion to closure in order to move on with my day. Fathers, on the other hand, want quick, bottom-line sound bites.

So, when asked for a super quick summary of our Student Mastery Program, I respond: motivation plus study skills.

When parents want us to really describe how we do our work, I suggest that one part of what we do is "technical" and one part is "art." Teaching study skills – the technical part – is fairly easy to convey. We teach the best practices for student effectiveness. Getting students to do what they should do is the art of our work.

It is art not due to extraordinary creativity or brilliance, but rather that such work is too complex to explain in sound bites. The subjective, qualitative aspects of changing someone's psychology have nuances and subtleties too numerous and diverse to describe in simple narrative form.

Stories often provide a better way to explain.

"Can you help my son?"

This is the question that I am most often asked.

Jake's mom called with that question to start my day a few years ago. She continued: "He's bright, but not motivated and he doesn't have study skills. I have done everything possible to help. Nothing seems to work."

He's On A Downward Trend

Soon thereafter, I met Jake. Through middle school, he had done well: a mixture of As and Bs. 9th grade led to more Bs than As, and his first Cs.

Subject	Grade
Math	B
English	C+
Science	B
Language	B-
History	C+

Jake was now in the middle of 10th grade. He was getting Bs in math and science, despite habitually losing a half-grade for not turning in a few homework assignments each marking period. Jake's C+ grades in English and history made no sense to anyone who spent time conversing with him. His quick wit, ability to make connections, and capacity to discuss complex subjects – of interest to him – made it hard to believe that someone so verbally adroit performed so poorly in liberal arts classes.

He's distracted in class.

Jake did not pay attention in most of his classes. After a few minutes of listening to his teacher, Jake reported that he would "go somewhere else in his mind." Such mind-drifting happens to many students. But, for Jake, paying attention to his inner chatter was his primary state. His notebooks were filled with his doodling or funny notes to his friends. In addition, he confessed that he had mastered the ability to play a video game on his phone outside the attention of most of his teachers. He was also a mild discipline problem. Fortunately, his behavioral issues were more related to talking to his friends than being disrespectful.

As would be expected, his class participation grades were low. Also, given his nearly useless notes, Jake was at a huge disadvantage when he had to prepare for tests that relied heavily on paying attention in class.

He's too bored to study effectively

Jake's ability to focus while studying was even worse. His parents were quite strict and enforced a lengthy study period at home. By the time we met, his parents had already gone through the obvious methods to prevent distraction. They had taken away the TV in his room, prohibited him from texting while studying, and enforced a non-computer policy unless essential to homework.

Jake's parents had done exactly what they should have done. Yet, their efforts were to no avail. Jake would sit in his room and find ways to distract himself.

Is he just lazy?

Jake's grandmother concluded that he was simply lazy. His mother agreed that his actions could be interpreted as signs of laziness, but she never felt that was an apt term.

After conducting an assessment of Jake, I agreed. As is the case with most boys of Jake's type, those I will call Adventure Boys, laziness, as in lethargy, is not an accurate description.

Indeed, the opposite is usually true of Adventure Boys. They have enormous amounts of energy. Jake demonstrated this extraordinary energy when he was interested in either a subject or an activity. In science, Jake would perform brilliantly on the rare occasions when projects required building of any sort. Building, as a theme, was a consistent source of motivational energy for Jake. From The Pinewood Derby to science fairs,

Jake had always gone way beyond what was expected when he had what could be called "design control."

Jake also showed this energy in sports. He was an excellent basketball player. He excelled in the free-flowing parts of the game. He had been a star in middle school when the game was mostly unstructured. His high school coach, who ran a more structured offense, did not appreciate Jake's free flowing ways. The coach grew fed up with Jake after one too many improvisations. He told Jake that, despite being one of the top players on the team, he would not be a starter. He would play Jake when he sensed that the team needed a boost of energy.

He's not interested in the college process.

While Jake was certain that he would go to college, he had no interest in discussing college and would just nod or mumble when the subject came up. His parents noted that he did not understand how much his sub-par grades would hinder his college choices.

Jake's mom was really worried that the time to turn things around was running out. She was right.

Understanding Jake

When Jake met me, he was naturally wary of another authority figure being introduced into his life. Yet, he was also tired of underperforming. As he noted in his first conversation, "I'm smart, but my grades don't show it, and I'm a good basketball player, but my playing time doesn't show it."

After going through my rapport-building reassurance that I was simply there to help him, not evaluate him – and certainly not boss him around – Jake eased up and provided some very candid commentaries about his challenges.

In relation to studying, Jake would head to his room as directed, but he could not bring himself to study. He would organize his desk. He would straighten out his room. He would "do nothing" for minutes at a time. He would start reading one of his magazines as these were the only real tangible distraction left in his room. He barely enjoyed these activities, but simply could not bring himself to study in efficient fashion.

When he finally got around to studying, as much as 45 minutes would have been wasted. When he started studying, his thoughts would drift. He sometimes would stare into space or get up and shoot his Nerf basketball. Typically, his assignments should have taken an hour or two to complete. It would take Jake three hours. Subsequently, he grew to hate studying.

Identifying Jake's motivational pattern

There are general principles that will be relayed on how to best motivate your son. The most effective principle — communicating effectively within his motivational pattern — will emerge only after understanding your son's distinct psychological profile. You then will be able to push the right motivational triggers based on how he listens and internally processes your message.

Understanding Jake's type had been on my mind from the moment that I first spoke with his mom. Jake was an Adventure Boy, my own term for teen boys who could be categorized as Point Sevens within a psychological profiling system called The Enneagram.

I knew that I had to focus on "freedom and fun" to have any chance of shifting this Adventure Boy's motivation level. For students interested in doing well for the sake of public approval (such as those that I will call "Star Boys"), or in the hopes of connecting with their parents, peers, or teachers ("Social Boys"), or to feel in control ("Boss Boys"), or to feel special ("Drama Boys"), or to simply avoid conflict ("Go With The Flow Boys") there would be different ways to communicate this information than what I will specifically suggest for Adventure Boys.

Jake and I began discussing his life from a broader perspective. He thought school work was pointless. Unlike other types that might have the same view, but will do their work despite their misgivings, Adventure Boys like Jake will rebel. Jake's rebellion was less aggressive than others of his type, but nonetheless, his inability to get started with studying was his subconscious way of rebelling.

What was he rebelling against? Loss of freedom. Loss of fun. Jake did not like the thought that he was "missing out" on fun that he could be having instead of doing his homework.

We began to discuss Jake's bigger vision of his post high school life. He had heard his parents' repetitive warnings about not being able to get into a good college with his poor grades and that not getting into a good college would prevent him from getting a good job. He was certain that I was going to begin this oft-repeated refrain.

Yet teen boys, like most everyone, are far easier to motivate if they convince themselves of whatever point you want to make.

Creating A Vision

I simply asked Jake what he would find *fun* to do for work someday. Jake started with the normal adolescent response, a mumbled "I don't really know." Still, his parents' pestering had done some good by forcing him to give a little thought to the question. He wanted to "make cool stuff like Apple or be part of something like Google."

"What would be *fun* about that?" To translate teen-speak, Jake saw possibilities for companies he could start based on his long-standing passion for building and his newly found interest in technology.

Jake also thought it would be great to make "boat loads of money," but not because he cared that much about being rich, he claimed, but rather because he wanted to work when he wanted to work, and have fun when he wanted to have fun.

To plug into his vision and help him see the steps that could lead to making that happen, we looked up the backgrounds of employees who worked at companies that interested Jake. While there were exceptions, most of the high level employees, and in particular the senior executives and engineers, attended top notch undergraduate universities.

"Why do you think this is the case?" I asked Jake. He pointed out that good colleges serve as screening devices for companies like Apple that receive thousands of applicants every day. Jake said, "It is a lot easier to hire a guy from M.I.T. than some small state college."

We then reviewed the colleges of some of the engineering powerhouses that seemed to recur in the backgrounds of these employees.

In particular, we focused on the class percentile rank of the admitted students. Almost all of the students were in the top 10% of their high school class. "They must be getting As in English as well as math." Jake said it before I did.

Using Motivational Triggers

We talked some more about his vision and I focused on the *fun* of his potential work and the *freedom* that could come after working hard to build his career.

I then asked him whether he was looking forward to college. "I don't know. My parents say it will be a lot of work." True, but I wondered if he had a real sense of how most college students spend their days.

Shifting the vision of college life

Jake was not excited about college for several reasons.

First, discussions about college were not about college life, but rather the work needed to get into college. That is hardly inspiring. It would be like focusing on the hassles of plane travel when discussing a vacation to Disney World.

Second, his parents had warned Jake repeatedly that college would be much harder than high school. That made Jake view college solely as a place with an increased work load. Sticking with the Disney analogy, this would be like telling someone about the lines for the rides, but not about the rides themselves.

Third, college, as he was told, was one step closer to the "real world" and his parents emphasized that real world jobs were even more freedom constraining and fun draining than the rigid structure of school.

I asked Jake if he thought anything about college would be fun.

Jake knew that college kids woke up later than he did and had some sense that they "partied" more than high school students. Even so, he was surprised when I presented the following rough estimates of high school versus college life:

Comparison	High School	College
Wake up time	6-7 am	9-10
Average class hours per day	7	3
Busy Work Per Day	2-3 hours	Not much
Daily Socializing	Not much	A lot!
Going out	1-2x per week	2-4x per week

Sometimes parents misinterpret the claim about busy work as a suggestion that college students do not work as hard. "Busy work" as in daily homework is not a big part of college life. Mundane tasks such as completing math worksheets, studying for vocabulary quizzes, and writing out conjugations of Spanish verbs are the grind of high school work-life. This rigorous, tedious, and monotonous work comprises the bulk of what most teen boys cannot stand about school.

College students work equally hard, but in a different way: highly focused, engaged work for big projects, papers, and tests. They study a great deal, particularly around mid-terms and finals, but most college students can escape the high school daily routine of completing worksheets and other uninspiring school assignments.

In addition, Jake was happy to hear that he could have the freedom to choose many of his classes, to focus his studies in an area of his interest, and to socialize when he pleased. He, of course, loved hearing that most American colleges provide more opportunities for fun than any work or school structure known to mankind!

Certainly, we discussed behaving responsibly within the context of those expansive boundaries. Still, Jake's lack of interest in discussing college had shifted as he focused on the *fun* and *freedom* in college rather than the work and drudgery.

The college process could be viewed as enjoyable shopping

Jake's lack of interest in the college process primarily stemmed from the negative associations of anything related to college discussions. Whenever college was discussed, his parents would chime in that "he did not study enough and that with his grades, he would not get in anywhere good."

Why would he want to discuss the college process?

I showed him a college book that contained descriptions of over 2,000 colleges. I asked Jake to think about the college process from a different perspective.

Did he like to shop – at least in relation to something he wanted?

There are thousands of schools to consider "buying." Right now, he was in control of the shopping process. He could select which schools that he might want to attend. In addition, for the time being, I wanted him to focus on schools that he might like and where he had a fairly good chance at admission. This created a sense of positive expectation.

Jake loved the shopping metaphor in comparison to the "you better work hard or you will fail" manner that college had been presented to him. We found several colleges that seemed attractive enough for Jake to be excited about exploring and within striking range of his admissions possibilities.

Connecting boring present work to an exciting future vision

Now that Jake had his vision at least partially in place, we needed to connect his uninteresting work activities to a bigger vision. Adventure Boys, despite their natural disdain for constraint, can work well in structure if the tasks are connected to a powerful vision of freedom and fun. They also work better when the activity has a high degree of intensity.

For example, freedom and fun loving Adventure Boys are among the most common enlistees in the military. This paradox is explained by the military's ability to connect tedious tasks to the vision of being part of a team of brother warriors. That's the easiest way to explain how one gets an 18-year-old wild man to scrub floors with a tooth brush.

Further, the intensity of the work structure provides motivation in and of itself. I'm sure many negative adjectives are used to describe getting up at 5 a.m. for highly engaged physical fitness, but I am certain that "boring" is not one of them.

Adventure Boys need to have their work linked to a compelling vision, and they work best when forced to work with intensity.

While this book is not designed to provide full detail on the nuts and bolts of our Student Mastery program, certain techniques are vital for understanding how to motivate Adventure Boys.

Regarding Jake, we had to figure out how to connect the future vision of "fun and freedom" to the present work that he viewed as "boring and constrained." Also, we needed to increase his intensity in his present work in order to shift from boring and constrained to engaged, even if not enjoyable.

Increasing Test Preparation Intensity

In Jake's case, presenting techniques for shifting his boredom was as critical to his long term success as the big picture shift in motivation.

We started with our process called *"Guess the Test."*

Jake's method of studying was similar to most students: he "looked through his book and notes." This passive way of studying is ineffective and inefficient. And perhaps most damning for an Adventure Boy, it is boring.

Jake had a history test the next day and said he had studied already. He had his history book with him. I grabbed it and told him to take out a blank piece of paper.

I quickly wrote ten bold terms from the book on the board and said, "Test time!"

Jake evaluated whether I was serious and then attempted to define the terms that I wrote on the board. He could identify 6 of them accurately; had some idea about 2 of the terms; and no idea about the last 2.

I provided the definitions of the 4 that he missed and asked him to repeat the definitions.

Next, I wrote the ten terms on the board again. This time Jake answered 8 correctly and missed 2. We repeated the process until Jake answered all ten correctly.

I explained to Jake that the passive way he had been studying was not only ineffective, but also the culprit for causing boredom. Simply looking at the book and rereading information was mind-numbingly dull.

Much like intense exercise, taking tests might not be enjoyable, but the engaged energy that testing demands eliminates boredom. From now on, I told Jake he should do the following in relation to every potential test:

1. Create a practice test based on his knowledge of what would be on his test.
2. Take the test.
3. Study his mistakes.
4. Retake the test.
5. Repeat as necessary with a focus on testing past mistakes.

Increasing classroom intensity

Jake had to shift his abilities in other areas as well.

I started with class room participation.

The Learning Consultants has employed over 50 tutors in our company's existence. Many were full time teachers. I would often ask how they graded classroom participation. Each teacher gave me different answers.

Given that classroom participation often accounts for as much as 10% of a student's grade, it seemed important to figure out how to instruct students to excel in this area. Since evaluation criteria varied from teacher to teacher, we concluded that "classroom participation" is a subjective judgment. For that reason, general principles of excellence, as opposed to specific objectives, would have to be conveyed to students.

I showed Jake a chart that conveys one such principle:

Active Positive

- Participates by answering and asking questions
- Appears pleasant/happy and eager to learn
- Pays attention through making eye contact
- Increases the positive energy in the class

Active Negative

- Disruptive
- Interferes with the learning process
- Talks out of turn
- Jokes inappropriately
- Class clown but not in a pleasant way

Passive Positive

- Pays attention
- Answers when called upon
- Occasionally volunteers

Passive Negative

- Appears bored and sleepy
- Not disruptive but clearly not paying attention
- Grumbles or whines when work is assigned

Teachers might have different words for each category and many students do not neatly fit into only one box. Yet in general, those with traits in the Active Positive category get the highest classroom participation points, and those in the Active Negative get the lowest. Depending on the class, Jake usually was somewhere in between Passive and Active Negative.

I asked Jake to consider when he enjoyed his classes. He had to think for a while, but on the rare occasion when he liked class, he was involved in the discussion.

As a generic proposition, when energy is directed into something, attention (and fun) increase. For Adventure Boys, shifting of energy is vital for success.

I asked Jake to do the following: in his next history class, raise his hand to either ask or answer a question as soon as appropriate. In doing so, I assured him that his energy would be directed in the class rather than toward the inevitable mind drift or chattering with his friends. I also told him that it would be important to get involved as early as possible because it would be very difficult to get involved after he had already drifted. I emphasized that he should focus not on doing well in class participation, but rather having positive fun in class.

Jake had some reservations. He did not want to look like he was trying to "kiss up" to the teachers. I understood, but I suggested that he try to be brave and give it a shot. To his credit, he did. Jake reported back that on the few instances when he did what I asked, he enjoyed himself more. And, of course, he was beginning the transition toward better class participation grades.

Increasing studying intensity

As for studying, Adventure Boys need intensity. I suggested that he learn to shift his intensity through a technique that I call a "study burst."

The passivity of work creates boredom and inefficiency. Most people, and teen boys more than others, work in moderately-engaged fashion since working intensely is challenging.

Students need to learn how to shift their energy for tasks they do not like. We all have the capacity to shift our energy. Athletes and theatre performers provide the most common examples. When feeling under the weather or fatigued, performers will pump themselves up. They will mentally do their best to shift their energy from tired and unengaged to energized and engaged. Most students do not think of studying or test-taking in the same way as they think of performing. We change this view.

With a study burst, for example, we use a stop watch. We tell our students that they need to focus for 10 minutes as intensely as possible. We then tell them to think about how they feel during a test – particularly a test in which they have mastered the material. Most students are not enjoying themselves during a test, but they also are not bored.

When Jake and I initially tried this technique, he thought his first assignment was going to take 40 minutes. I told him that I expected him to get it done in the next ten minutes. This was not an assignment that required complex problem solving. It was classic busy work – the type of work that Jake hated. He seemed to think my expectations were crazy, but, when I hit the stopwatch and said "go," he got to work. And he did what I asked – he worked with intensity.

10 minutes passed. Jake was astonished when he realized that he had completed nearly 80% of the assignment. He was so happy that he asked me to give him a few more minutes to finish the whole thing – which he did in another 5 minutes. What he thought would be a 40 minute busy work assignment was done in 15 minutes.

Jake gained 25 more minutes of fun! And, at least with this busy work, quality did not suffer.

I asked Jake if we could break down his normal way of working. He reported that it would take him 5 to 10 minutes simply to get started. He would get bored during the assignment and not really push himself to finish his work efficiently. He would almost always get up and take a break after 15 minutes. He would then have a hard time restarting.

Jake was attracted to the energy involved in study bursts and he understood that he could add to his fun time by working more efficiently.

The Paradigm Shift

Jake did not change instantly. His parents said that he saved his best moments for our sessions. But a few weeks into our work, we had a conversation that led to Jake's longer lasting transformational moment.

We both happened to have watched a documentary on the Navy SEALs. The program depicted the intense training that these warriors endure. Jake was very inspired. He had no interest in going to the military, but he said he wanted to push himself to the limit.

Jake was OK with my philosophical ramblings, so I broke into my "personal movie" speech.

People feel inspired when they come out of movie focused on a main character who overcomes an obstacle to reach a big goal. There is a generation of men who still run up stairs after watching *Rocky*.

However, few people are involved in situations as dramatic as those portrayed in the movies. Life's inspirational moments are more subtle. Indeed, the moments of life in which most people are pushed to their limits often do not feel inspiring in the moment. Staying up all night with a sick child or working overtime all weekend to complete a work project are the times when we adults are reaching our potential. Without reflection, these periods just feel like moments that we want to end.

This is the case with students as well. Studying 3 hours for a chemistry test after a grueling soccer game or preparing for AP exams, SATs, and finals simultaneously are the Navy SEAL moments in a student's life.

"Do you understand, Jake? This is your movie. You are the main character. But, your Navy SEAL challenge is not diving into freezing water and doing sit-ups on the beach at 2 in the morning. Your challenge is doing your homework every day. That is how you will make the most of your potential right now."

While this speech might not work with many young adults, it resonated with Jake. "So what I hate doing is actually my Navy SEAL thing."

Yes, exactly, Jake. Exactly.

Behavioral Change

Jake's story was not a straight line to success. His compliance was far from 100% with the variety of strategies and tactics suggested. Yet something shifted in him. His sophomore year grades increased across the board, but not dramatically. He suggested, and I agreed, that his teachers had already formed an opinion of him and that it was an uphill battle to shake their already formed impression, particularly in relation to classroom participation. And, of course, his bad habits were hard to instantly shake off. Still, he was changing.

Most importantly, he had stopped his downward trend and moved the arrow in the right direction.

It was during junior year that Jake's performance took off. After visiting a few colleges, the escape that college represented in the specific form of his top choices became the distinct, tangible vision for which he was willing to sacrifice. He started referring to "doing the Navy SEAL thing" when we would see each other.

I made sure that every discussion focused on the *freedom* and *fun* that college represented. The motivational imprinting was the link between his Navy SEAL thing and the *freedom* and *fun* that the colleges of his desires represented.

Jake's junior year grades shot up.

Subject	Grade
Math	A-
English	B+
Science	A
Language	B+
History	B+

He also dug in for SAT prep and scored high 600s in math and low 600s in reading and writing.

Jake wound up attending an excellent undergraduate business school that had a specialization in technology. When

I last heard from him, he was having a great deal of fun while getting solid grades and excitedly creating a business plan for a national competition. His passion for building was now becoming a passion to build businesses.

How did you inspire my unmotivated son?

This is the second question that I am most often asked. Many parents have graciously asked if I could bottle up the magic and give it to them. I wish it were that easy.

It isn't, but if you follow what I suggest, I hope that other parents will soon ask you – *how did you inspire your son?*

Chapter Two

The Three Paths

Why does motivation matter more than ever?

The simple answer is that the future work world will be extremely great for some; a struggle for many; and truly horrible for others.

From a big picture perspective, the new work world is nothing like the 1950s through the early 1990s where relatively stable work structures made for a predictable career landscape. We are in a period that is more like the Industrial Revolution on steroids. Back then, few knew that the world of work was forever changing. This was an auspicious time for smart, hard working, young men who amassed fortunes as they seized new opportunities. But those who did not prepare themselves adequately for the shifting work world found their way of life rocked.

We are in a time of similar economic turbulence. Why is it that some boys will be thriving in spectacular fashion in a few years, while many will be struggling with the masses or living at home?

Your Son's Three Future Paths

Given the massive economic shifts taking place, your son will be headed toward one of these general paths:

Abundance: a path of abundance marked by great fortune economically, with vast opportunities to gain significant wealth at a young age, and psychologically, with vast opportunities for extraordinarily enjoyable and fulfilling work, along with optimal work-life balance, or . . .

Struggle: a path of struggle, marked by job instability and more time working for less money, or . . .

Disaster: a path of disaster where financial independence is out of reach.

Abundance	Struggle	Disaster
• Excellent work character	• Average work character	• Poor work character
• Top Skills	• Average skills	• Poor skills
• Top Credentials =	• Average credentials=	• Poor credentials =
• Great job or great entrepreneurial possibilities	• Tough job prospects	• Highly limited job prospects

The Path of Abundance

Where there is great transformation, there is great opportunity.

Those who capitalized at the start of the Industrial Revolution became the richest men of their day. Those who led the computer and various Internet revolutions did so similarly. Every sweeping change creates abundance for the first to understand how to benefit from the change.

Chaos creates opportunity.

We are in the midst of economic-work-job chaos. The work life for most of your sons will barely resemble what you faced when you started your career. This puts many parents in the same position as the family farmer at the turn of the 20th century watching their son head into the city for a job at the factory.

Some of you may be in companies (Intel) or industries (search engine optimization) or work structures (free-lancers) where the beginnings of these transformative changes have already taken place. You know what I mean from an experiential viewpoint. The rest of you surely can see that the predictable work landscape of post-WWII through the late 1990s is already gone.

We are just at the beginning of this new world of work. The changes to come, due to even more radical globalization and break-through technologies, will be more rapid and dynamic than even the massive changes of the last decades.

So why could this be potentially wonderful for your son?

Your son could develop a combination of outstanding skills, credentials, contacts, and work character. He will be in a position to make his work life creative, enjoyable, fulfilling, and prosperous.

He will have periods of intense yet engaging work. And if he succeeds, he will also have the choice, at a far younger age than you had, to spend time traveling, engaging passionately in his hobbies, being with his family, and living an ideal balance of work and personal life. He will have abundance of both time and money.

Potentially, your son could develop a work life with far greater freedom than you would have believed possible when you started your first job. While *The Four Hour Work Week* paints too rosy a picture of this world, Tim Ferriss did a great job of showing what kind of work life can be created by the talented.[2] As the title suggests, your son could be entering a work world that you might consider unrealistically great – as in working four hours per week while earning a substantial income. He could potentially leverage technology and modern work structures to have prosperity of both money and time at a very young age. He could choose to "retire" before 40, maybe even 30. Given his potential for "acquiring" abundant free time, he might organize a charitable foundation, develop his artistic talents, travel the world, and/or just stay home as much as possible with his growing family. He also might have so many creative, inspiring, and interesting projects that he'll choose to work intensely, partially for more money, but also for the challenge of reaching his human potential.

How could such a great work world exist? The boundaries that required the majority of younger workers to wait for decades before capitalizing on their talent have been broken down. The tales of the Google-Facebook-Twitter-YouTube guys have become cliché. The more interesting story is of the thousands of young men who are doing the same, albeit in a less sensational way.

There have always been young men who had great ideas, but in most cases, capital was needed to have such things as office space, equipment, labor, inventory, and every other part of infrastructure that was required to make the great idea become a reality. For that reason, most young men went to work for others and let their ideas wither away.

Today in part, and in the near future in an exponentially bigger way, your son will need the intangibles of a great idea, excellent work character, communication skills, problem-solving ability, social connections, credentials to help make connections, and . . . that's about it. Other than a

---

[2] Tim Ferriss, the author, created a company that provided significant passive income and through the use of new technology and virtual staffing allowed him to work about 4 hours per week. Even if he is exaggerating, Ferriss seems to have a great work life and significant spare time to engage in numerous hobbies.

computer and a few other low cost technology items, there is no longer a need for expensive infrastructure. If he has sufficient *work character*, a theme that we will explore in greater depth, he will be able to leverage such things as cloud computing, virtual (and cheap) labor, his social media network, and every other non-physical component that now enables ideas to become reality.

In addition, the talented in creative fields, technology, and finance (among other areas) will be increasingly able to demand a premium for their services well beyond what would be expected given their experience.

Since their work will largely emanate from their own interests, the likelihood that they will be highly engaged and passionate about their work is much higher than ever.

Moreover, given the disappearing need for face time, your son will be able to be with his family, develop his hobbies, and balance his life in way that that every overworked corporate and professional achiever in the last generation never could.

In this new world, your creative and talented son will have enormous creative control over his work and personal life. Great fortune, economically and psychologically, awaits him.

The Path of Struggle

Others will not be so lucky. They will face the new world of work where tumultuous instability is the norm. This already seems to be the case in many industries. Many will face permanent job insecurity. They will be forced to switch jobs every couple of years and switch career tracks as needed. Those on the path of struggle will face great financial hardship when their employment is yanked from them at inopportune times.

For those on the path of struggle, the need to jump from job to job due to outsourcing, downsizing, contract ending, company closing, and all other destabilizing economic shifts will be standard fare.

A smaller portion of this struggling group will have what are considered good jobs and stable careers. But they will work extraordinarily hard to maintain a similar standard of living as their parents.

This will include many professionals. Relatively speaking, this sub-group of those on the path of struggle will be fine financially. They will simply make the trade that many generations have done before them: a lot of time for a lot of money. Yet the trade-off will not be as fortunate as it was in the past.

Even for the talented, the globalization of the world's labor markets will deflate wages for most Westerners. The same forces that decimated the US manufacturing sector will soon do the same to the lower level white collar world. If a large accounting firm can hire a smart, hard working, non-American to crunch numbers for half the price, well, that is exactly what it will do.

Metaphorically, the C-student accountants who formerly had lower level financial jobs will have difficulty securing employment. The B students will be employable, but will likely face downward salary pressure due to the same deflationary pressures of worldwide competition. Only the A students with excellent work character will avoid long stretches of time on this path.

The Path of Disaster

Some portion of your son's generation will suffer deeply. They will suffer in a way that no other generation of children from the middle class has since The Great Depression. They will have long periods of unemployment interspersed with periods of unfulfilling work. They will likely need the financial help of their parents well into their thirties. Thereafter, they will barely be able to sustain themselves let alone a family of their own.

In addition to the aforementioned macro-economic shifts, they will not have developed the work character required for the new world of work. Many will have been raised with an "everyone gets a ribbon" mindset, but they are heading into a brutally efficient Darwinian job market. *The lack of being properly motivated to build their work character* will be the root reason why they did not develop the skills, credentials and contacts necessary to prosper in the new world of work.

In school, they will have done the bare minimum to get passed through, but they will not have developed a sufficient work ethic, let alone high level writing, reading, and problem-solving skills. They will neither be able to build their credentials nor be able to develop meaningful professional contacts. This will make it impossible to compete for high-end white collar jobs.

More significantly, they will face ruthlessly inexpensive worldwide competition for lower paying white collar jobs.

What about blue collar jobs? There have always been young men who floundered academically. Their physicality was their primary job skill. That was fine when we had a strong manufacturing sector, but many blue collar jobs have largely disappeared along with the manufacturing sector.[3] Facing a work world that demands high level education, yet having under-developed communication and problem solving skills, a deplorable work ethic, and inadequate credentials they will be shell shocked to discover that they are not entitled to anything in the work world. No ribbon. No job.

Fortunately, your son has a parent like you who will steer him clear of the path of disaster, help him through the path of struggle, and lead him to the path of abundance.[4]

How will you do so?

---

[3] The trades are not part of this analysis. Talented electricians, carpenters, plumbers etc. will be in great demand for the foreseeable future. While higher education is not a necessary component for those in the trades, work character is still the key for success.

[4] If interested in greater detail regarding the future career paths facing your son's generation, see Appendix B for further articles.

You will learn how to motivate him to reach his potential.

While this book will focus on education, the more important issue will be how you can learn to motivate your son to develop the work character necessary for success.

And, guess what? You are your son's best and possibly only hope.

Chapter Three

Student Mastery's
General Principles

The heart of this book focuses upon specific motivational paradigms that will help you inspire your unique son to success, but there are general principles that set the foundation for ensuring such success. While I will address some commonly held wisdom, I will try to focus on areas that might be reasonably new to you.

Motivating You

If you are reading this book, you are plenty motivated, at least compared to other parents. Still, you need to ready yourself for battle. After several years of nagging to seemingly no avail, most parents give up. You will persevere.

You have decided to learn whatever is necessary to ensure that your son succeeds.

You are willing to face more mumbling, grumbling, and grunting. You are committing to push yourself through being ignored, disrespected, and manipulated.

Finally, you are readying yourself for more grueling combat with your son's peers, societal influences, and hi-tech distractions.

As for those distractions, your generation might have been equally disdainful of authority and similarly influenced by bad peer groups, but today's diversions are of a different magnitude. In retrospect, your distractions were not that interesting. *Three's Company?*

Now, consider what your son experiences:

1. the capacity to maintain anytime, anywhere social communication through social media, texting, and live interactive game play;
2. instant access to customized media options through YouTube, DVRs, and downloaded videos;
3. captivating video game systems that make Space Invaders seem like tic-tac-toe.

Even the television and the phone, your main distractions from your teen years, have morphed into multi-functional entertainment magnets.

You will need persistence to muster the energy required to monitor your son's daily activities, push his specific motivational triggers, and guide him through the peaks and valleys inherent in any change.

Most all parents want to help their children, but few take the time to learn how. Your help is more necessary than ever. We are facing a combination of pervasive male underachievement and massive macroeconomic shifts. This is creating a permanent cycle of underachievement for young men.

You want to help your son in school. This is the near-term goal.

The long-term vision is even more important, as your son's young adult future hangs in the balance based on his teen years. My hope is that this book will help you put your son on the path toward a fulfilling life.

While this book will only touch upon specific tactics within our Student Mastery Program, several principles provide the philosophical foundation.

Principle 1: You Are Chief Education Officer

When you grew up, the school system had a near monopoly on design control of your education. Your parents likely ensured that you did your homework and studied when necessary. Maybe they punished you when you did poorly and rewarded you when you did well. Yet your parents probably did not spend much time figuring out how to best educate you. That was the school system's job.

Now, it's your job. Here's why:

If I argued that the school system is broken, I am not sure who would argue back. Indeed, stating that "something is really wrong with our education system" meets with the rare case of unanimity among all sides of the political and philosophical spectrums. There are disagreements about who or what is to blame, but I have not heard anyone in recent years argue the broad point.

Your involvement in your child's health care provides a useful comparison to what is now demanded in education. When parents (almost always mothers!) put their child into "the health care system," they do not turn into passive spectators. They do whatever they can to ensure that their child gets the best possible health care in and out of the system.

After their child leaves the doctor's office, parents ensure that the patient-child does what he should in order to get healthier. Most parents research illnesses, evaluate alternative treatments, consider options for what is ideal, and then actively make decisions to serve their child. This process is particularly true of parents of children with chronic illnesses. The parents often become experts on the illness. In doing so, they become the de facto chief medical officer of their children's health.

Similarly, you must become the chief education officer of your children's education.

As life-long learners, we all would do well to master the craft of "student," but your son has the formal job of "student" for at least 17 years (assuming he attends college). He might have that job for 19-21 years if we add in graduate school and/or the increasingly prevalent 5th year of college. That's likely the longest job he'll ever hold. Yet there is no job training for "student."

Your son attends classes in different subjects. His teachers instruct in math, English, history, and so forth. Some provide suggestions on how to study for their courses. But other than distributing minimalist and unread study suggestion handbooks, schools do not train students in the best practices of being a student. Some students have natural work habits that help them succeed. Others are self-taught or have parents who teach them how to be a student. Most, however, have no real methodology for student success. Parents have to figure out how to fill this void.

The Greater Need for Parent Involvement

Malcolm Gladwell, the noted social commentator of *Tipping Point*, *Blink*, and *Outliers* fame describes a research study of children in Baltimore.[5] The study was designed to figure out why children from wealthier family backgrounds performed better than those from impoverished families. Prior to the study, some thought genes or the educational background of the parents would be the determining factors. Neither was most significant.

The critical difference: how much students developed academically *during the summer*. Who is in charge of student's education in the summer? Parents.

---

[5]   In the *The Outliers*, Gladwell wonderfully addresses the issue of mastery as well as the issue of education. As would be expected, it turns out that most every "outlier" – those who have achieved mastery beyond any normal curve – may have developed genius, but, only genius after a lot of focused, intense work. 10,000 hours seems to be a general standard threshold for attaining mastery.

The researchers discovered that the correlation with wealth and academic accomplishment is not about wealth at all, but rather parental involvement in providing additional educational opportunities. Wealth made it easier to provide such opportunities, and thus from a macro perspective, led to greater achievement.[6]

The detail of the study revealed that children from lower economic backgrounds learned at an equal rate as their wealthier counterparts during the school year. For that reason, each group tested nearly equally during the first couple of years of schooling. The noticeable differences in achievement started showing up thereafter. That was curious to the researchers. Differences in genes or parental educational background would presumably have an equal effect on 1st graders as on 4th graders.

The students were consistently measured to determine how much they improved during the school year. For the most part, the findings stayed the same: the parental income of students had no effect during the school year.

However, the achievement gap kept increasing each year. It was then that they realized that those from wealthier families ·learned more in the summer.

So, for example, Student Affluent and Student Impoverished had equal achievement at the end of 1st grade, but Student Affluent's parents were able to enforce self-study, send their child to enrichment camps, and obtain tutoring. These parents generally served as Chief Education Officers in the summer. Student Impoverished's parents were generally not in the position to do any of those things.

It does need to be emphasized that there was no data to indicate that this was a reflection of values. Instead, the lack of involvement emanated due to lack of resources – both

---

6   I feel the need to comment from my own observations: plenty of parents without much money figure out how to provide additional educational opportunities and plenty of parents with a lot of money do nothing to enrich their children's education.

economic and energetic. Many families from the lower end of the economic strata were headed by single parents. Most of these working parents had neither the economic resources to pay for academic enrichment nor the energy to meaningfully educate their child. They were, after all, doing their best to provide economic sustenance for their families.

As the years passed, Student Affluent's summers of enrichment gradually shifted the achievement gap between the two students to greater proportions.

Gladwell pointed to another finding of equally significant dimensions for parental involvement: when reviewing students from countries that performed well on international education tests, the length of the student's school year was the most dominant factor that predicted success. US students spend about 180 days in school. Several Asian countries – including those whose students crushed US students in international education tests — have 220 to 240 school days per year.[7] Parental involvement in education during non-school days is the only way to close that differential.

Prior to global workforce competition, the achievement gap between US students and others would not likely lead to a significant future impact. As the world has become "flat",[8] our students are competing against international competition. Students from other countries are working 20-30% longer each school year. As the years pass, they are outdistancing the normal American school child. Your son will be facing that competition when he graduates. Only you will be in the position to ensure that he is prepared.

Principle 2: Build Work Character

Parents will often ask what they should do to help their children. Develop their math skills? Enhance their writing

---

[7] http://4brevard.com/choice/international-test-scores.htm

[8] See Thomas Friedman's seminal work *The World Is Flat* on our interconnected world.

abilities? Teach Chinese? Do whatever possible to gain admission to an Ivy League school?

Build their work character is my response.

Work character could be viewed as the "it" or "X" factor that separates those who succeed and those who do not. This attribute goes beyond simply working hard. The subtleties and nuances of work character encompass a myriad of factors including the willingness to work long hours, work intensely, figure out what work is needed to be done, do work that is necessary but not enjoyable, work as much as is necessary to accomplish a goal, work as much as possible without knowing with certainty that a goal will be accomplished, and simply "doing what it takes" to achieve a goal.

Several abilities illustrate the general concept of work character.

The ability to defer gratification

Many of you have heard of the marshmallow experiment. I'll briefly recap here. The Stanford marshmallow experiment – repeated in dozens of variations in different settings – offered small children, presumably of the normal sugar craving variety, the following proposition:

After placing one marshmallow in front of the child, the experimenter would say that she was going to leave the room. The child could eat the marshmallow immediately or wait until the experimenter came back. If the child waited for her to return, he would get two marshmallows.

The study was originally designed simply to examine when children develop the ability to defer immediate gratification of a small reward in order to obtain a bigger reward. It was, however, the longitudinal study that created the experiment's fame.

Through the years, the researchers conducted follow-up studies. They discovered that those who had waited for the second marshmallow — thereby demonstrating the ability to defer gratification — had obtained success at a statistically significant rate compared to those that immediately gobbled up the first marshmallow.

Not to worry if you think your teen boy would not have fared well on this test when he was a toddler. This is a skill that can be developed and might even be a skill that your son has demonstrated in other areas. For example, young athletes will engage in training activities, such as wind sprints, that capture the essence of deferred gratification — doing something not enjoyable in the present in order to get a bigger reward thereafter. Such training illustrates their capacity for deferring gratification. I tell students that the same person who is willing to run up and down hills to get in shape for football can implement this trait for academics.

The ability to deal effectively with the uncomfortable

This principle applies to both parents and children alike. Parents need to force their children to do things that they do not like to do. That's not fun. No one wants to be the nag, the bad boss. Yet compelling your son to dig in and work, even when he does not want to work, is (contrary to some strand of crazy, modern parenting) necessary for most teen boys.

Here, some parents seem to forget that most adults, left to their own volition, will choose fun over work. Remember that if your bosses or clients or bills did not compel you to forego fun for work, you, too, would be socializing more often.

Those who think that teens will choose to master what is necessary to succeed in school probably have not spent much time with teens. While it is true that many children want to learn, they quite naturally want to learn subject matter that interests them. The drudgery of school, the busy work, the structure, and the constant testing are all tough. It makes the entire school process uncomfortable.

To an extent, I agree with some of the complaints: the amount of generic and uninspiring content and the mountain of busy work required are among the numerous areas which illustrate that our educational system needs massive repair. That's a different book. This book is about how your son will deal with "what is." And your son must master "what is" in order to reach his bigger goals.

Part of "what is" is dealing with the uncomfortable. I tell students that if they can do the work (studying subjects of minimal interest) that they do not like now, then they'll be able to do the work (within their preferred college major-career path) that they like later. Life becomes easier after learning to deal with the uncomfortable.

The ability to work despite the ambiguity of potential results

I know this sounds a bit high-brow, but it's the most accurate way to convey that when teen boys realize that they are not automatically guaranteed success for their efforts, they will not work as hard. Ambiguity is a motivational deflator.

I tell students: "I wish I could say with certainty that if you do what I suggest then you will gain admission to the college of your dreams, but I can't."

Why does this matter? Kids deal with far more angst than most parents realize. I have had dozens of young adults say to me that they worry if they work hard and don't achieve a good result (either top grades or admission to a choice college), then they will feel bad that they "wasted their time studying when they could have had fun."

By the way, it is highly likely that your children will never convey these thoughts to you. They fully understand the 20 minute tirade that will likely follow. So, they keep such thoughts to themselves.

Most actions-rewards for young people work within the behaviorism construct – good actions yield rewards. Do your chores, get your allowance.

From that perspective, good input guarantees a known and immediate good output. But getting top grades or admission into a desired college has a far lengthier distance between action and reward. More significantly, the reward is not definite.

Studying in high school does not guarantee As. In addition, there is no guarantee that studying hard and getting As will lead to admission to a college of choice.

As soon as students begin to realize that their work efforts do not automatically lead to good results, many suffer the same angst as adults do when in similar situations. For example, some of you likely are in an organization that does not seem to reward hard work. In such places, motivation suffers. Adults think: "Why does working hard matter?"

Teen boys are no different.

The ability to develop habits of excellence

Francie, my wife, makes each of our children participate in swim team during the summer. None of my three kids will swim competitively in any other context. But Francie's view is simple: swim team builds character through forcing students into the habit of dealing with the uncomfortable.

The swim coach is a gruff, tough, blunt-speaking woman who does not tolerate whining and makes the kids get into the outdoor pool regardless of how tired and cold they are on sometimes chilly Connecticut mornings. The kids who stay with the team develop the habit of going into the pool regardless of how they feel.

So it is with students who are compelled to develop habits of studying. I often cringe when I hear 17-year-old high school juniors tell me that they have "a policy" of not studying on weekends. Had they developed a habit of studying on weekends, they never would have formulated such a self-defeating policy.

Students who follow our Student Mastery Program will hear the phrase "habits of excellence" repeatedly. While we are not militaristic in our approach, we do advise that mastery in most areas emanates from following the same procedures repeatedly.

For example, we strongly urge that our students put study routines into place during the weekdays. The routine might have a distinct time slots such as: "5 p.m. – study begins." Or the routine might simply follow a process: "Upon returning from soccer, I shower, eat, and then study." On the weekends, we compel students to commit to a distinct "power hour" of studying such as 11-12 on Sundays. Parents usually must monitor and enforce these suggestions to build the habits.

Work character emerges through developing habits of excellence. As an educator, I enjoy working with any disciplined performer. Swimmers, long distance runners, and ballerinas (among others) have developed the habit of working through the uncomfortable. They have seen the results of dealing with challenging drudgery in order to obtain rewards thereafter.

The old time advice that "you should send your son to the military to make a man out of him" is actually very solid. The armed forces develop habits of excellence that create long lasting character.

Principle 3: Move your son from being outer- to self-directed

Simply put: your son needs to become self-motivated so you can stop nagging him. Good luck! This is unquestionably the hardest challenge known to any coach, teacher, and parent.

How can you create a vision that permeates both the brain and the heart?

How can you move your son's subconscious so that he starts to make good choices automatically, without nagging?

The second half of this book addresses these questions squarely by teaching how to motivate your son based on his specific type.

But first, we'll start with some general guidance.

Moving from an Intellectual to an Emotional Understanding

To understand how to motivate someone, you need to first understand the difference between an *intellectual and an emotional understanding*.[9] For example, your son might "get it" that he needs to have better grades in the same way that a dieter understands she should avoid chocolate chip cookies.

For many, however, an intellectual understanding does not change behavior until there is a compelling emotional vision that is connected to the change — such as a dieter who is emotionally invested in wearing a bikini to the beach.

For the special few, the vision of gaining high honors or being in the top 10% of their class or simply the picturing a report card filled with As will be sufficient. Yet for the majority of teen boys, the emotional desire for obtaining good grades usually emerges if and when they feel that they have a connection to something tangible. The desire to attend a specific college or the generic "good college"[10] seems to be the most concrete.

With that said, even the majority of teen boys entering 11th grade find college too distant to meaningfully motivate them. The challenge, as we will discuss, is to make thoughts about college more appealing.

I wish this was not so. It would be wonderfully refreshing if abstractions such as striving for self-actualization, reaching one's highest human potential, and learning for the sake of

---

[9]   *Switch* by Chip and Dan Heath provides the best explanation that I have ever seen on this point and many others. A must read for anyone interested in motivation.

[10]   That phrase "good college" means all sorts of things to different people. Whatever that means to your son – use it!

learning would shift teen boys. Unfortunately, with limited exceptions, such philosophical exhortations will fall flat.

There is a way to leverage teen self-absorption, however.

Use the Older-wiser self dialogue

One exercise that I have found works surprisingly well for vision creation is the Older-Wiser Self Dialogue.

I started using this technique as a way of helping students become more self-directed. Teen boys have tuned out their parents' lectures and most assuredly would tune out mine.

So, in an effort to get them to lecture themselves, I ask them to picture speaking to an older version of themselves – usually just a couple of years older. It turns out that teens are more interested in their future than you would have thought.

"What would an older-wiser you say to you today"?

Years ago, I worried that this question would come across as one of those geeky things that a stereotypical counselor would ask, but I have been astonished by the general response.

Your grunting teen boy who seemingly only thinks deeply about how he will advance his video-gaming skills is also "coming of age." To a parent, growing children are often frozen in an earlier age. But your evolving boy is now half-kid, half-adult — and when asked to access his adult side, he might pleasantly surprise you.

He might actually have given some thought to the future. He might not have ever discussed his thoughts because he may have interpreted your questions about the future as a form of nagging.

Further, in all likelihood, he will initially rebuff your question about his older self, but he might actually give the question some thought thereafter.

The question is, after all, an interesting one. I have had numerous students tell me that they have asked themselves, "What will an older me say to me?" during critical junctures in their lives.

Regardless, the question starts to change the dynamic from you nagging your son about the future to your son talking to himself about the future.

In this discussion, I then move from the abstract to the concrete.

I try to impress on my 15-year-old students that creating college choice may not be particularly meaningful for them today, but as 17 year olds, they will be leaving high school and will want to control that change.

I use varied metaphors to convey this message. Some students have switched schools due to moving or transferring to private schools. They understand such a change affects choice of friends, activities, and academics (and, yes, choice of friends seems to have the most impact). I explain how college choice is even more significant than high school choice, but that this time they will have power over controlling the choice.

For others, I pose hypothetical scenarios that illustrate why they will want the capacity to choose. "You will work at McDonald's if it will help get you that Jeep."

I continue: "While you do not know what it is that you want after you leave high school, you will agree that your older self will want something. And, he will either be very mad at the current version of you for not putting him in position to get what he wants or very happy that you worked hard to give him the chance to control his future."

Ultimately, the Socratic dialogue boils down to a phrase that students cannot argue with: "You will want what you want. So you may as well do what is necessary to get whatever it is that you will soon desire."

Even the toughest teen boys have nodded in agreement over different versions of this speech.

PART II

Chapter Four

The Patterns

Speak To Me In My Language

When I first started the work of The Learning Consultants, I met Chris as he was finishing up his freshman year of high school. Funny, engaging, and quick witted, Chris made a great first impression. His interests at the time were very normal: sports, social life, and video games. He was a good athlete, popular, and, if it can be considered a talent, good at Halo, his video game of choice at the time.

I met Chris as a referral from the parents of his friend Doug. Doug and Chris were best friends. The same adjectives that described Chris applied equally to Doug. He was similarly athletic, popular, and, for what it's worth, a good Halo player. Since they looked reasonably alike, called each other "bro" incessantly, and played lacrosse, their classmates called them the "Lax Twins."

Academically, they were similar as well. They had solid Connecticut Mastery Test scores, but their grades were a mixture of Bs and Cs. They were both viewed as underachievers academically, but they were doing wonderfully well in the areas that mattered most to them: sports and social life.

Our company was hired to train them in smart study techniques and to help bolster their grades in their subject areas of challenge. The approach was similar for both, and the number of meetings with each was relatively equal. Both improved their grades at roughly the same clip and wound up freshman year without any Cs.

I heard from Doug's parents during mid-October of sophomore year. Doug's progress reports were not good. We needed to work with him again. We did. And, his grades improved. We did not hear from Chris's parents until March. "Chris is having a good year, but could benefit from one of your talks."

At the end of sophomore year, Chris finished with mostly As and some Bs. Doug made all Bs, but just barely.

There were similar variations of this pattern during junior year: I met with both Doug and Chris. I would meet with Doug because his performance was spotty. I met with Chris less frequently and usually only for what his parents would call "one of our talks." Chris no longer needed to work with us regularly, as he was a straight-A student and seemed to have his study habits down. His parents, however, suggested — and Chris agreed — that his energy would shift after our meetings.

While I knew what Chris's mom meant by one of our talks, I had not yet fully realized that these talks were the reason for our better results with Chris than Doug.

I then reflected on the success of some of our other successful clients. I realized that I was engaging with them at a different level than with other students. While I tried to motivate all of our students to do what we asked, some – the ones that were the greatest successes – were being motivated in a more profound way.

I understood Chris's psychological attractions fairly well and would appeal to him that future conventional success, something that he cared very much about, would depend on his present grades.

In a later chapter, I will discuss a pattern that I call "Star Boys" and their intense attraction to public approval. Their academic challenges often stem from seeking public approval through sports and social life at the expense of school. In fact, if Star Boys perceive getting good grades as having a negative social impact, they often will self-sabotage their chance at academic success.

With Chris, there were a few turning point conversations, one of which was the "video game" discussion. I am not an old crank who hates video games. I think the brilliance of new video game technology is the reason why video games are a problem. X-box, the Wii, and whatever game system soon surpasses them are amazing.

Chris candidly admitted that he knew he spent too much time playing video games at the expense of studying. I agreed that these game systems are captivating, and could see why he enjoyed the playing different games so much.

I seemingly changed the subject by asking him, "In the eyes of others, what makes someone at your age *successful*?" He responded that the basics were having a lot of friends, demonstrating athletic talent, and doing well in school.

"How about being good at video games?" I asked. He conceded that, while there was social trash-talk related to video game talent, being good at video games was not part of the success package and that being bad at video games would not be perceived as failure.

What would be considered high school *failure?* The first thing Chris mentioned was not getting into a "decent college."

So, I started my cross-examination.

Am I correct that playing video games has nothing to do with *success*, but that doing well in school has a lot to do with *success?*

Is it true that you could be viewed as a *failure* if you do not get good grades, but playing video games poorly has nothing to do with whether you are viewed as a *failure*?

The conversation went on in this fashion until Chris started laughing at "how stupid it was" to spend so much time playing video games. When later hearing the story, Chris's mother almost fell over because she had been trying to make the same point for several years, but to no effect.

Over the next few meetings, we had big picture discussions regarding college and career. We had conversations about partying and other social distractions. The *success* and *failure* buttons were pushed and pushed and pushed. Chris would perk up in these conversations. He was interested in *success* now, but was also out to ensure his *success* later. Chris's intensity was ignited. He became a self-motivated student. His parents rarely ever had to nag him again about his school work.

I had, in broad strokes, discussed some of the same issues with Doug. But Doug never seemed that interested. I thought about my discussions with Doug. We would do our work, and during the time that we were not focused on the task at hand, we had light, fun conversations about sports and his crazy high school adventures.

I would try to have similar conversations about success and failure. Our video game conversation started as mine had with Chris, but Doug kept on focusing on the present *fun* of video games over the future success of college admission. In addition, the lack of *freedom* required to do his homework seemed to be a bigger fear than failure.

I thought about Doug and realized that despite his outward similarities to Chris he was really a different psychological type. At this point in my work, I had read a great deal about different personality profiling systems and realized that there was something about psychological patterns that really mattered.

In this case, Doug was one of those Adventure Boys, mentioned earlier in Jake's story. Energetically, he seemed similar to Chris because both Adventure and Star Boys tend to be extroverted, athletic, and engaging. But the types are different in some fundamental ways. Adventure Boys are most attracted to *fun* and *freedom*. Their biggest fear is being trapped by a constraining structure.

Sure, Adventure Boys are interested in public approval and conventional success, but these motivational triggers are far less significant to them than for Star Boys. Adventure Boys are more attracted to *fun* and *freedom*.

I should have been selling Doug the *fun* and *freedom* he would have in choosing a college and the *fun* and *freedom* that college presents. While his grades improved marginally, I had failed in my efforts to profoundly shift him. Fortunately, Doug's reasonable grades and stand out lacrosse playing helped him gain admission to a solid college.

I heard from Doug's mom after his freshman year in college. He was repeating his high school pattern. He did well enough in classes that he liked. He had mediocre grades in his other classes. She wondered if I could give him one of those "talks" that seemed to work so well for Chris, who just finished a great first year at a top notch university.

I was delighted to have a second chance.

Doug was not as cheerful as I remembered. Thoughts of the real world, post graduation, were getting him down. "I can't see myself sitting in some office all day like my Dad."

Doug's interpretation that he should get good grades so he could get a good job was having a deflationary motivational effect. Doug did not want a "good job" like his Dad, an executive in the pharmaceutical industry.

Freedom and *fun* were psychological triggers to press. And, in Doug's case, he wanted to make a lot of money so he could have control over his freedom and fun.

Since this was during Wall Street's bull days, I asked him if he'd ever considered becoming a stock broker. He liked his finance class and he particularly liked the one unit on the stock market. He was part of a team that picked a mock stock portfolio. He liked watching the market's twists and turns. "It was kind of fun, like gambling."

Doug had never considered becoming a stock broker because he figured that it was just like one of those office jobs he did not want. I explained to him that the job of a stock broker has morphed into different variations of financial sales specialists and wealth managers. These jobs require high energy, demand quick action, and reward thick skin. Adventure Boys usually have skills that match these prerequisites. And, at least pre-Great Recession, many successful financial sales specialists became wealthy at a fairly young age. Potentially, lots of fun and lots of freedom awaited him!

All this sounded great to Doug. His mood had noticeably changed and he said he felt hopeful about the future of work for the first time.

There was a catch, however. To get one of those jobs, without connections, Doug had to build a resume that would make him attractive enough to get his foot in the door. Other than through internships and otherwise demonstrating an interest in finance, getting good grades was the only way to help him gain entry to Wall Street.

Doug understood.

I did not hear from Doug for several years. He then called regarding GMAT prep as he was planning to get his MBA. He thanked me for our past meeting and briefly recapped his last three years of college and his first year at work. Not only had Doug turned his undergraduate performance around, he had landed a job selling annuities for a large financial institution. Even better, Doug thought that there were bigger things in store for him if he got his graduate degree in business. He noted that it was hard to believe that he wanted to go back to school, but he enjoyed his classes once he had control over his course selection and a destination to head. His classes were no longer prison cells, but rather part of his route to freedom.

I do not view our single interaction as the event that magically transformed Doug. Perhaps I simply pointed him a direction that he would have discovered on his own. In addition, Doug had the good fortune of being naturally funny and quick-witted, skills that are huge assets for a salesperson of any sort. I'm sure his interviews went well.

In any case, I know that motivation – and specifically motivation related to his type – was the missing piece of his academic success puzzle.

I had begun to realize that if I understood the patterns of my students, I could press on their specific motivational triggers in order to help them reach their potential.

As for Chris, I recently was on a large e-mail blast from a very proud mom trumpeting his graduation from medical school.

Chapter Five

Personality Profiling

The Persona Behind The Personality

Since the remainder of the book will focus on using motivational communication triggers based on your son's psychological pattern, I feel compelled to comment on personality profiling.

Some people love the concept of personality theory. If you do, you can likely skim or skip through this chapter. You might be more interested in getting right to the "how to help your unique son" part of the book.

Others scoff at the personality theory and particularly tests that determine personality types. If you do, or are skeptical of such tests, then read on. I am entirely cultured in the scientific method and trained as an attorney. I find truth through factual observation of evidence and approach new ideas with a healthy degree of skepticism. I am neutral regarding my embrace of any personality test including ones that I currently use. I am a pragmatist, not an ideologue. If someone showed me a better tool than any that I employ, I would have no interest in defending the instrument, but rather would try the new one.

I do understand criticisms of many personality tests. I think many are at best fun, but superficial. There are only a few that deserve serious attention. Regardless, I have a different take on what should be criticized. The sham web ads that try to sell a personality test – even valid ones — usually suggest that the test will provide an answer, usually to a big question such as career or marital choice.

Even the best tests do not provide such answers. Instead, these tests provide data. That data is only useful if turned into helpful information, and then only actionable if the information is turned into good advice.

For that reason, personality test results are only useful, as opposed to merely fun, if you know how to turn the data into helpful information and subsequently use that information for guidance, or if someone with expertise can provide the same.

Simply put, *personality tests should be starting, not finishing, points.*

For example, if you took a personality test that revealed that you are pessimistic by nature, you might say, "Well, I knew that already. So what?" But if you took the test as part of a career counseling session and you were considering a job that involved sales, it would be helpful to know that most successful salespeople are more optimistic than normal. They need to be ever hopeful. Successful salespeople often have to present to 10 or 20 or 50 people before they make a successful sale. Optimism is required to keep making those calls. Competent career counselors would take that simple data point regarding pessimism, provide you information regarding the fit for sales, and presumably advise you that a job that requires a lot of selling is likely not well suited for you.

Turning test data into helpful information is what successful advisors do for their clients, and what you should do for your son if you want to use personality theory successfully.

Some additional points for skeptics to consider:

1. You may have taken a personality profiling test that had little scientific or historical validity. There are thousands

of such tests proliferating on the web. That you took a test created by a charlatan does not invalidate all tests.

2. If you had a valid test, it is quite possible that you had a poor administrator or interpreter. That the administrator did not effectively gather data, or that the interpreter of the data did not properly counsel you, does not invalidate effective personality tests.

3. It is highly likely that you were not instructed or did not know what to do with the results of the test. This would cause frustration if you were expecting "an answer."

For example, someone in his mid-twenties recently came to me for a career counseling session. Unrelated to our work, he had taken a career inventory test that provided recommendations regarding careers to explore ranging from machine operator to airline pilot. He complained that such expansive recommendations did not help him find his career. However, I suggested that the test showed that he really desires a more engaging, action-oriented job.

The data needed to be transformed into information. For example, the capacity to move around would be vital for his job satisfaction.

This information needed to be turned into advice. He had come to us due to his ambivalence about seeking to leave his secure job. He was miserable in his current work. However, his co-workers with the same job chided him for complaining, as they liked the work sufficiently. They had convinced him that he was being childish, so he had resigned himself to staying put.

I explained that being stuck in an office staring at insurance data all day was not tortuous to his co-workers. I would guess that many of them probably liked the data analysis and detailed review required in the job. Personality preference tests would likely reveal that they enjoyed the secure feelings of staying in one place and performing detailed analysis. They likely felt comfortable and confident in mastering a job that required excellence in repetition. Security in both structure and activities would likely be important for them. My client, however, needed to leave before his life was sucked out from him.

Further, those who resist personality theory do not like the thought that something as vast as human personality can be neatly put in a box. I fully agree. For example, the values within a culture or a family are of enormous influence on one's personality and psychology. Most tests do not have enough questions that bring out the import of this factor.

As illustration, someone who derives great satisfaction from public approval will present very differently based on cultural upbringing. In cultures where modesty is more highly valued than in the United States, the brash conceit demonstrated by many American public figures would not be tolerated. So, those who are "Star Boys", my nickname for teen boys who are primarily driven by gaining public approval, will act differently based on their heritage.

Moreover, the psychological/interpersonal development of the individual tested creates vast differences in how the "boxes" should be interpreted. For instance, someone who is declared "extroverted" could be an engaging conversationalist who has developed excellent listening skills or an annoying, attention-seeking, non-stop blabbermouth.

Indeed, I would say that the psychological development of different individuals who test similarly is the biggest reason why valid personality tests are misinterpreted. When two people of varied states of psychological health are put into the same category, the person on the higher end will naturally think "I'm not like her!"

Nonetheless, some personality systems, when understood and applied properly, can provide excellent insight.

The Enneagram

At some point in law school, I became acquainted with the Enneagram. For fun, I took the questionnaire to determine my type. I found it accurate as did those in the group who similarly typed themselves. But it was not until I gave the Enneagram test to a different friend that I took a deeper interest. The test unveiled what I thought was a surprising result. His outward personality did not match his type, or so I first thought. Then I considered the matter further, and almost like the scene in *The Usual Suspects* when Keyser Soze is revealed, my friend's façade had been unmasked. I had a clear recognition that the test uncovered his motivational make-up. It seemed that the test understood him better than I did.

The Enneagram seemed to go far deeper than any test I had seen in uncovering one's psychological archetype. I soon learned that I was not alone in this view. While the Enneagram, along with most personality tests, has its share of critics, it has been gathering enormous momentum through the business and psychological worlds. Even stodgy corporate America, including AT&T, Boeing Corporation, The DuPont Company, General Mills Corporation, General Motors, General Mills, Kodak, Hewlett Packard, Toyota, Procter & Gamble, and so forth have used the Enneagram.

Similarly, higher education and government have embraced the test. For example, Stanford University's Business School had a course for its students based entirely on the Enneagram. And the organization with the world's highest need to understand people – the CIA – has used the Enneagram to help understand world leaders.

For me, the most powerful moment of external validation regarding the system occurred in my discussions with my friend, Dr. Andrew Hahn. Unrelated to my own discovery of the Enneagram's usefulness, Dr. Hahn, a world renowned psychologist, had embraced the Enneagram as a primary tool for understanding people. Since I have never met anyone who understood people as well as Dr. Hahn, I felt even more confident that this was a methodology that I should master.

The Enneagram's growing popularity stems from its ability to uncover our emotional core. This core might be described as our primary motivations. These motivations lead us to patterns of thought, action, and style. It is a great system, but I emphasize that I am only interested in using this tool as one way to uncover core motivations. I am not selling the Enneagram as "the system" to use.[11]

What does core motivation mean?

We have conversational ways of discussing the dominant motivational drivers in people: "he needs to feel special and unique," "she needs control," "he never make waves," and so forth. Yet most of us do not have a system that explains the significance of these drivers and how we can benefit from understanding them.

In relation to motivation, "understanding why" someone acts is far more revealing than "how" someone acts.

The Enneagram identifies nine core personality types which are known consistently by their Point Numbers. Non-Enneagram purists give nicknames that attempt to conversationally capture the type:

---

[11] In my experience, the Enneagram has proven to be the most effective personality profiling tool for uncovering core motivational patterns. But I have found other systems, such as Myers-Briggs, extremely effective in other areas. This is not a claim that the Enneagram is the best overall system, but rather that it is useful for figuring out how to optimally communicate motivational messages. I also have my own problems with the test. The complexity of the Enneagram makes it a very challenging system for most people to understand. That's a weakness, not from a theoretical perspective, but from a practical one. In addition, some of the criticisms of the Enneagram on a theoretical level give me pause to embrace it wholeheartedly. But it turns out, from my experience, that the system works. That's all that matters to me.

T: Nickname Quick Description	Major Indicators
Point One: The Perfectionist	principled; rule-oriented ; rigid; self-critical
Point Two: The Giver	relationship-oriented; caring; people pleasing; jealous
Point Three: The Performer	high achieving, adaptable, vain, image-oriented
Point Four: The Romantic	expressive; creative; moody; melancholic
Point Five: The Observer	perceptive; objective; emotionally distant
Point Six: The Skeptic	responsible; committed; fearful; anxious
Point Seven: The Adventurer	spontaneous, versatile, bored easily, callous
Point Eight: The Boss	confident; decisive; controlling, "bossy"
Point Nine: The Mediator	agreeable; easy to be around: not sure of own needs; malleable

This simplistic chart does not convey the power of the system, and even within the system, I recognize that:

(1) humans are far too complex to put in boxes,
(2) none of us "always" acts in a defined manner, and
(3) each point's stereotypical strengths and weaknesses vary from person to person.

Degrees of Emotional Development

There are also clear degrees of psychological development that dramatically affect how each presents. Someone who is a Point 8, known as "The Boss" will almost invariably come across as direct and straightforward regardless of personal development. But a well-developed Boss might be thought of as an inspiring and strong leader. General Norman Schwarzkopf, from the 1990's Gulf War, serves as a likely example of a healthy Point 8. A less developed Boss might come across as imperial and controlling. Here, Tony Soprano comes to mind.

I have noticed that image-oriented people have great resistance to the Enneagram. Unlike other tests that focus on the superlatives of the type, the Enneagram focuses more on the psychological challenges of each type. So, for example, typical Myers-Briggs descriptions extol the gifts of each type. I am an ENFJ. I love reading about my type, and if you know your Myers-Briggs type, you will enjoy reading about your strengths.

However, such information is not always that helpful, and is almost always not fully honest. If only I could be as good as that description.

The Enneagram strips away false fronts, but this naturally creates some negative reception amongst people who have spent time building their façade.

How is such knowledge applied?

In working with adults in career counseling, many have said "that explains a lot" as a way of expressing the feeling one gets after a deep psychological insight. Since self-awareness is a major key to both personal and professional success, many Enneagram test-takers delve into studying the system in order to learn more about themselves and others important in their lives.[12] In working with students – and more importantly to you in working with your son – it becomes a deep way to understand how to motivate him to reach his potential.

The following cannot be emphasized enough: the most important lesson that this book will convey is *the need for you to figure out how to communicate with your son through his unique psychological make-up*. You do not need the Enneagram or any other system to do so. I would guess that most every effective athletic coach through history never used a personality profiling system, and I'm sure that many parents do not need a system to understand their unique child.[13]

The Case Studies

Before we get to the patterns, I want to be clear that the vignettes in these successful case studies do not fully capture the messiness of reality. I am bundling up a case study in a few pages. The time line from struggle to motivational epiphany to success may appear to be quick and a straight upward path. Motivating others rarely works in such fashion. Plenty of students take a long time to change. In addition, most

---

[12]   I'll jump off the Enneagram train at this point, at least for purposes of this book. There are a variety of modern spiritual seekers who use the Enneagram for personal growth. The intention of this book is neither to lead the reader toward or away from that direction. This book is completely focused on motivating your son in a *practical* way.

[13]   This book uses the Enneagram as its base system, but is not about the Enneagram for several reasons: My focus is on helping parents motivate their children, not on explaining the highly complex Enneagram system. I use the Enneagram as an instrument to help explain how parents should leverage their understanding of their son's motivational framework to shift their motivational energy. If you have different instruments or simply a different sense as to how to best approach your son in this manner, I urge you to take the general thesis of the book – *raise your son's intensity through pressing his unique motivational triggers* – and use whatever methods you think are most effective. Further, this book focuses on a very small subset of people – high school boys in suburban America related to a very small subset of issues – motivation related to practical success within this age group. The Enneagram's applicability to all people and all issues is not the focus of this book.

students – even those mentioned in the case studies – had an upward-downward-upward fluctuation. And, of course, I have changed names and non-consequential biographical data in order to protect the privacy of our clients.

As a parent dedicated to changing your son's life, you have a lifetime job. I hope this advice will serve you throughout your career.

Chapter Six

Typing Your Teen Boy

Do your best to think of your son in relation to the world – not simply in relation to you.

For example, it could be said that most every teen boy wants more freedom in relation to his parents. But consider the issue from a broader perspective. Is freedom his dominant focus, or is it control, or is it public approval? Is your son consumed with public approval from a conventional perspective, or does he want approval for being unique? These subtle differences are important in sorting out his dominant motivational pattern.

Which statement describes your son best?

With 1 being first and 9 being last, rate these statements in order.

Questionnaire 1

Type	Statement	Order
P	My son follows the rules.	
G	My son focuses on relationships.	
S	My son cares about public approval.	
R	My son wants to be unique.	
O	My son wants to acquire knowledge.	
W	My son worries.	
A	My son wants freedom.	

B	My son wants control.	
M	My son wants to relax.	

Questionnaire 2

Which group of adjectives describes your son best?
With 1 being first and 9 being last, rate these statements in order.

Type	Adjectives	Order
P	Perfectionist-Rule Follower –Rigid	
G	Giver-People-oriented-Jealous	
S	Performer-Achiever-Inauthentic	
R	Romantic-Moody-Dramatic	
O	Observer-Introverted-Nerdy	
W	Skeptical-Loyal-Worrier	
A	Adventurer-Energetic-Unfocused	
B	Bossy-Dominant-Strong	
M	Mediator-Goes with the Flow-Calm	

Questionnaire 3

With 1 being first and 9 being last, which scenario best depicts your son's high school life?

Type	High School Life	Order
P	Rarely gets in trouble, nice group of friends, does his homework, studies but is inefficient and seems to procrastinate	
G	Interested in being liked; values friendships; girlfriends; distracted socially; does not get in much trouble except for talking too much in class	

Type	High School Life	Order
S	Focuses on standing out either socially or athletically, is either conventionally popular, stars in some public endeavor or is frustrated in not succeeding enough	
R	Different than typical boys, moody, alternates between being sensitive and self-absorbed, off beat sense of humor, involved in the arts	
O	Studious with good grades; one or two good friends, not popular by high school definition, if distracted from school work, the distractions emanate from his own interests	
W	Good student who worries over his grades; cynical sense of humor, small but loyal group of friends	
A	"Spirited" (the nice way of saying "wild") group of friends or he is the "spirited", upbeat, one in a group of friends; not interested in doing his homework or anything that he views as boring; discipline issues have arisen throughout his school career; shows spurts of high energy towards his interests	
B	One of the leaders of his social group; if involved in school activities, holds leadership position; often engaged in conflict	
M	Group-oriented but more as part of the pack and not as the leader; not intense about his school work or activities, likes to "hang out" a great deal	

Add up your scores and arrange in numerical order.

Letter	Type	Order
P	Perfect Boy	
G	Social Boy	
S	Star Boy	
R	Dreamer Boy	
O	Observer Boy	
W	Worry Boy	
A	Adventure Boy	
B	Boss Boy	
M	Go With The Flow Boy	

It is highly likely that your son is one of the top two types. It is highly unlikely that he is anything on the lower half of your scale. Upon reading the case studies, you will likely have a more precise sense of his type.

I am sure that those versed in personality profiling will note that the simplicity of these questionnaires will surely create some mistyping. Guilty as charged, but I also am fully aware of the "busyness" of parents and have used this quick form to successfully type 95% of teens.

From here, all the case studies should be helpful, but you are most interested in the type of your son. Go right to that type and start getting precise help.

PART III

Chapter Seven

Go With The Flow Boy

I just want to relax.

Brief Description

If you can picture your son relaxing on the couch when you leave the house for work and be in the same position 8 hours later when you return, you might have a Go With The Flow Boy. Lacking in intensity, Go With The Flow Boys do not cause many problems due to their actions. Instead, their problems slowly creep up due to their inaction.

Go With the Flow Boys do not push themselves to excel in areas that are not inherently enjoyable. Parents usually report that Go With The Flow Boys seem to hang out a great deal, either doing not much of anything or spending an inordinate amount of time engaged in their favorite multi-media activity.

While it might not be quite fair to call them followers rather than leaders, Go With The Flow Boys tend to be group-oriented, doing whatever it is that the group leaders want. Those who have an athletic peer group will play their sport of choice for hours. Being part of a group that focuses on video games and skate boarding is also part of this dynamic. The Go With The Flow types who have a peer group that does a whole lot of nothing quite often end up smoking a whole lot of pot.

The Psychological Pattern

Go With The Flow Boys rarely cause dramatic crises. Ironically, this makes their pattern one of the most dangerous. They do not get in much trouble – unless they are with a crowd that gets into trouble. They do not get Fs or do anything that causes significant conflict in the house. The danger is more like that faced by the proverbial frog in gradually boiling water.[14]

Go With The Flow Types avoid stress. From a positive perspective, they tend not to have much achievement neurosis. One way to avoid stress is to not strive, and Go With The Flow Boys are fine with not striving. Go With The Flow Boys will do enough "to get by." Stress from striving generates anxiety for them and so is avoided.

The Challenges

The original title of this book was *Raising Intensity*. It was created with Go With The Flow boys specifically in mind. No one needs their intensity raised more than Go With The Flow Boys. They display an emotional "flatness" in relation to school and productive endeavors. "Please energize my son!" is the battle cry of parents with this type.

Go With The Flow Boys drift into colleges, majors, and careers. They do not like making decisions about future choices because of the internal conflict that stems from making tough choices. They often will come up with a pat answer about their

---

[14] In case you do not know the reference, frogs placed in water will sit placidly even if the temperature slowly increases to the boiling point. They will be cooked alive because they do not observe the subtle, gradual shifts in their situation that eventually put them in peril.

college and career plans because it seems easier to have an answer than to simply say "I don't know."[15]

Big choices, such as college decisions, cause major challenges for Go With The Flow Boys. Since decisions cause inner conflict, they are particularly indecisive. For this reason, they often either avoid getting involved in the search or report that each of the colleges they visited seem fine. If they drift into the right college, then things will go swimmingly.

If not, Go With The Flow Boys do not will themselves to make the most of bad situations. Many of those young men in their early twenties who attended some college before dropping out, and who are now working at local minimum wage jobs and have no idea what to do with their lives, started out as Go With The Flow Boys.

The Hope

Lacking self-awareness, Go With The Flow Boys are perhaps the most in need of "waking up." If they start to understand themselves, and in particular, realize that they need to take greater control of their destiny, then they have perhaps the best of all worlds: trying to do their best without the neurosis that afflicts many achievers.

More particularly, our greatest successes have been in helping Go With The Flow Boys find the right path. When directed to a field of interest, Go With The Flow Boys do very well. They feel comfort in knowing they have found their direction, and with that comfort they are willing to do what is necessary to stay on track.

There is more good news for parents of this type. Go With The Flow Boys are almost always likeable. They do not have

---

[15] Since we live on the shoreline in Connecticut, I have noticed an awful lot of Go With The Flow types say "Marine Biology" when asked what they want to study. They are usually picturing a stress free life on a boat where they get to study sea creatures. I suggest they talk to real marine biologists who will dissuade them of this notion.

issues with authority, which saves parents from a lot of stress. Since they rarely make waves, they rarely cause drama. In addition, as they often can see both sides of issues, they are frequently called upon to mediate disputes and decisions within groups.

Further, while not having strong preferences is a challenge, not having strong distastes is a plus. Go With The Flow Boys are not picky. They can deal with many types of environments and situations. Indeed, "Go With The Flow" could be rephrased "Happy Go Lucky." And that's not a bad way to live.

Case Study

"Timmy's not a bad boy," his mom said. "He does what is asked of him. He goes to his room to study. I just think he's inefficient. He bombs big tests." Timmy's mom went on to report that his friends were not bad kids either, but that they just planted themselves on the couch for hours playing Call of Duty. She continued: "He doesn't have a lot of get up and go, and the only time he seems really engaged is when he's skiing."

Timmy's grades had what I considered the classic pattern of Go With The Flow Boys. His report cards did not indicate a straight downward line. Instead, each year, from 7th grade through 9th grade, Timmy's grades would become progressively worse until they reached a point where his parents would intervene more aggressively. Then, his grades would go up. But when it seemed like he had changed – and when his parents eased up on the pressure – Timmy's grades would decline again.

The nagging had become a source of strain in the house, prompting Timmy's mom and dad to have the classic parental debate: should we let him fall on his face to teach him a lesson (Dad's view) or intervene aggressively (Mom's view)? Letting students fail academically in high school most often leads to disaster. It was a good thing that Mom won out.

My first meeting with Timmy went as I had expected. He was a thoroughly pleasant young man, but he had not given too much thought to his future.

I figured that I would get directly to the point. I asked Timmy what motivated him to work. His answer: "to get my parents to stop nagging me."

Beyond having pegged him as a Go With The Flow Boy, Timmy's answer was expected for several reasons. First, simple detective skills could deduce that the pattern of his grade fluctuation directly correlated with the stress level that he was getting from home. Timmy's work ethic would slowly deteriorate until he reached a point that called for heavy parental intervention. When his parents became more involved, Timmy would increase his work ethic.

Second, my observation has been the following: Go With The Flow Boys will become more engaged when the stress level of not working harder is higher than the stress level of working harder.

To say it another way, Go With The Flow Boys are fine with minimal nagging. But once the intensity of the nagging reaches a point that creates anxiety, they will choose the lower anxiety associated with putting in a few more hours of homework.

We also discussed Timmy's penchant for "hanging out," not doing much of anything during unstructured time. In conjunction with his parents, we instituted a new routine. Prior to our interactions, Timmy would typically get home from school, get something to eat, play video games or go to his friend's house, and then come home for dinner. He would then do his homework and, if he had a big test, study. On the weekends, he would only do homework if it was due on Monday, or study if he had a big test on Monday. More often than not, it meant he did nothing productive on the weekends.

In our new routine, Timmy could have a break after school until 5 p.m. His parents usually had dinner around 6. So at 5 p.m., Timmy had to do his homework until dinner, using at least one "study burst" for 20 minutes. After dinner, Timmy had to study – whether or not he had a test – for at least two 40-minute blocks. On the weekends, he agreed to study from 5-6 p.m. on Sunday as his "power hour," and also another 40 minutes after dinner. We put his schedule together and required him to daily check off his process list. He was generally honest, so this monitoring could work.

Timmy no longer had to think about when he was supposed to do his work. Since Go With The Flow Boys work well when they do not have to spur themselves to action, we had put into place a structure that took out the daily decision of when he had to start work. He just had to follow the plan. Without such structure, Timmy would just hang out. Timmy's overall drive, or lack thereof, stayed about the same — but his grades improved with his new structure.

During a later meeting, I asked Timmy to pretend his parents did not care how he performed in school. What were his goals? He paused. Go With The Flow Boys do not often think about what they want. "I guess I would want to do pretty well." What does that mean? "I don't know. I guess I would want Bs." Why? Timmy paused again. "I guess for college." The truth was that he really had not given any of the questions much thought and was just giving me answers that he thought I would want to hear.

I then asked Timmy if he felt like he was just going through the motions at school. He affirmed. When do you feel most energized? "When I am skiing and hanging out with my friends." I asked rhetorically: Which feeling state is better? Passively going through the motions or being intensely engaged?

I explained to him that many people let life happen to them rather than create the life they wanted. I delicately suggested that he was on track to be one of those people unless he started doing things for his own reasons. Timmy nodded. Maybe he understood?

Timmy seemed at least somewhat motivated and he had a big test that week. Like most Go With The Flow Boys, Timmy did poorly on big tests. The reason was simple. He did not put information into his long-term memory. He did just enough to get decent grades on quizzes and tests related to a small amount of material. When he was tested on cumulative material, problems arose because he had not mastered his overall work. We did Guess The Test. This was the first time I had seen Timmy exhibit any intensity.

Timmy and I met several times to work directly on his homework, but some part of these meetings came back to that same theme: you need to become more involved with your life. After one of the last meetings, I went home a bit deflated. I thought *he's not going to change.*

At the start of the next meeting, Timmy interrupted me. This was a first as he usually said nothing unless prompted. "I feel like I'm waking up." I was happily surprised by the phrasing, as I had been using it with seemingly no impact over the preceding months. "I was sitting in history class yesterday and noticed that I was doing what you were saying about just existing. We were discussing World War II and I thought I am going to force myself to get more involved. So I asked the teacher why we dropped the second bomb on Japan. She seemed glad that I was interested and then we spent about 10 minutes discussing the issue. You were right. I enjoyed the class more when I was active."

Getting teen boys of any type to create a big picture vision is challenging (except perhaps for Dreamer Boys), but Go With The Flow Boys are the most difficult in this regard. I peppered Timmy with additional questions about what he wanted in life knowing full well that he had not given much thought to any of these issues and that having to think about the future would cause him some discomfort. Yet I also knew that he was in the beginning stages of becoming more self-aware and that he would not push himself to ask these questions. We then started discussing different ways that he could push himself to a higher level. It was a start.

Since Timmy really had no idea about what he wanted to do for his future career and which major he might pursue in college, we had a career counseling session. Through use of a career testing battery and discussion, he grew increasingly focused on computers and specifically computer programming. In addition to having a genuine interest in computers, Timmy seemed to really like the focus of developing expertise in one area. The specialization would provide a stable path and Timmy would not feel compelled to continually make career decisions.

Timmy was now on a path that he liked. Go With the Flow Boys like the comfort that such structure can provide. We examined colleges that had computer programming. Most every school required higher grades than Timmy had in the present. He knew he needed to work harder, and he remarked that now that he knew where he was heading, it made more sense for him to dive into his studies.

With a path in mind, a developing self-awareness, and a structure to follow, Timmy had awakened. He went on to unexpected scholastic success and acceptance into a college with an excellent computer programming department.

Action Steps

1. Do whatever possible to help create a distinct college and career path

Upon figuring out their path, Go With The Flow Boys can do extraordinarily well. Their path provides a comfort zone. In that peaceful place, they can work long hours, deal with teachers, get through mundane work, and do all the tedious things that other types detest.

2. Design a rigid work structure

Unlike other types who rebel against forced structure, Go With The Flow Boy do very well in structure. They no longer need to think about what to do, but rather follow a procedure.

Create a precise work schedule and precise work expectations. While definitely not true for other types, adherence to rigorous routine is often ideal for Go With The Flow Boys.

3. Monitor. Monitor! MONITOR!!!

Teen boys need to be monitored, but Go With The Flow Boys need parental involvement and accountability because their problems are undetected. Unlike other types that might rebel loudly against doing their work (Boss Boys) or become too distracted to do their work (Adventure Boys), Go With The Flow Boys will comply with study times. Left to their own devices, however, they will do enough to stay out of trouble and not much more.

Chapter Eight

Adventure Boys

Give me fun and freedom.

Brief Description

If you can picture your son in the old Mountain Dew commercial featuring a bunch of young men jumping out of planes and doing other crazy fun and freedom-oriented activities in an upbeat and out of control manner, then he is quite possibly an Adventure Boy. Many teen boys could be described as impulsive and easily distracted. Likewise, many detest structure, bore easily with tasks outside their areas of interest, and find school and studying constraining. Yet no other type has this set of issues converge with the quite the force that sets Adventure Boys into a category of their own.

On the surface, Adventure Boys are buoyant and full of energy. Either on the go or immersed in their favorite activity of the moment, Adventure Boys are thrill-seeking enthusiasts on a never ending quest to escape boredom. Some parents of Adventure Boys recall their craziest friend from high school and will say that it was lot more enjoyable having a friend with this personality type than a child with this type.

The Psychological Pattern

Adventure Boys want fun and freedom. They avoid the feeling of being trapped at every possible opportunity. Adventure Boys have clear attention span issues. In my observation, a disproportionate number of what I am calling Adventure Boys have actually been diagnosed with Attention Deficit Disorder, or its cousin, Attention Deficit Disorder with Hyperactivity. There are specific medicines and techniques that are generically employed by those with ADD and ADHD.[16] If that is the case with your son, certainly, use both medical and psychological science in conjunction with what I will suggest. I will stay singularly focused on how you, as a parent, can shift the motivation of such a student.

The positive spin regarding Adventure Boys – upbeat, fun-oriented, confident, and adventurous – sounds very appealing. The more challenging question is: Why are Adventure Boys so desperate for freedom? What are they fleeing from? It turns out that they are often not really escaping from anything outside themselves, but rather their own mind. Dealing with boredom and any negative states of emotion are more challenging for them than other types. This is a big problem for reasons that go well beyond school. Unfortunately, Adventure Boys are the most likely type to get into the troubles that most worry parents, such as extreme partying and wild behavior.

---

[16]   I do not know enough about the science of the brain to immerse myself in the debate on whether ADD-ADHD is over-diagnosed. I am certain that in many cases diagnosis and medication has proven to be helpful. I also know that some percentage of boys have always met the diagnostic criteria for ADD-ADHD. Perhaps they need medication to deal with the extreme structure of school. Or maybe the structure of school is the issue – at least for them – and nothing is really "wrong" with them. They are just wired differently.

The Challenges

Based on their general description and psychological pattern, it should be of no surprise that Adventure Boys have the largest general set of issues in relation to school. Their very nature rebels against the structure that is imposed on them.

When feeling trapped by such structure, Adventure Boys perpetually plan their escape in the form of diversion. Classrooms are one of those places with imposed-upon structure. In addition, most Adventure Boys have an anti-authority bent since authority figures represent the jailor. Their attraction to freedom and fun creates major problems when dealing with rules that restrict them. The combination of a desire to be free and inherent anti-authoritarianism usually means Adventure Boys will have discipline problems.

Studying poses similar challenges to Adventure Boys and more headache-inducing challenges for a parent. You are now in the position of jailor. Whatever can distract them will distract them and you have to be the monitor of their monkey minds. In addition, Adventure Boys are the most likely of all types to think that missing out on present fun is worse than working for future success. Adventure Boys might respond to the suggestion that they should stop doing what is fun in order to work for something that might lead to success as follows: Fun is success and there is no time better for success than now!

The Hope

Adventure Boys thrive on intensity. Their need to link work activities to an intense goal or purpose is critical. When the vision is in place, they can direct high energy to making the vision become reality.

Paradoxically, seemingly attention deficit Adventure Boys display extraordinary focus when they find an activity that engages them. Adventure Boys often immerse themselves in their new favorite activity. Their seeming devotion might last a week, a month, a year — and then just like that, they find a new activity to immerse themselves in and discard their last passion. It is, however, wonderful to see Adventure Boys who develop long-lasting passions because their energy leads them to great heights.

When they find something productive that engages them, Adventure Boys soar. If you can picture an amped-up technology start-up founder pitching his company's product with zany child-like enthusiasm,[17] then you can see one version of the hope. In addition, their very nature – optimistic and energized – makes them generally positively charged, even if only superficially. If they develop into more self-aware individuals, they have an outstanding mixture of natural cheer plus depth.

Case Study

"Should I get him tested?" Steve's mom said in our first phone conversation as she described him. She was referring to testing for ADD. She then detailed his normal way of being. He was engaging, but his eyes often darted around. He fidgeted incessantly, and his eagerness to move was ever present. "He can't sit still. We used to think this was normal for an energetic young boy. But he's 16 now."

Steve had always been a discipline problem in school. If he thought something would be funny, he would simply do it. Unlike Star Boys, who try to be funny to entertain their audiences, Adventure Boys are as focused on entertaining themselves as they are on entertaining their friends. Some teachers could handle his antics and found him fun, even if challenging. Others could not. In elementary school, he was in the principal's office on a near weekly basis. In middle school, he had been suspended

---

17   Star Boys could be pictured in similar vein but usually have a more focused, less crazed, demeanor.

for throwing soup at another table. In high school, he had been arrested for breaking into the school at night.

"But," his mom insisted, "he's actually kind hearted. He doesn't want to hurt anyone." The soup incident was just a friendly food fight that got out of control. The school break-in was based largely on a dare and he neither broke nor stole anything. Mom noted that his teachers usually liked him, but admitted some had to remove him from class because he was interrupting the learning process of others. At home, he would either claim he had done his homework in school or he would do his homework so quickly that his mom knew that it was not completed with quality.

Steve's mom thought his antics were in response to her home life. She had divorced Steve's dad when Steve was 3. Steve's dad had remarried, had a couple of children with his new wife, and moved to a different state. Steve saw his dad for two weeks in the summer and another week during school vacation. Steve's mom tolerated, if not condoned, Steve's behavior as a response to his father's absence.

When I met with Steve and discussed his family situation, I disagreed with his mom's assessment. His family situation did not seem to bother Steve that much. He only had sketchy memories of his Dad being part of the family and claimed that it was hard for him to miss what he never had. He said his dad was a "cool guy" and he did not seem to be angry with his Dad.[18]

Was Steve masking his pain? Maybe. And while I'm sure the divorce affected him, his father's absence, in my mind, was not the cause of his school challenges. His mom had viewed Steve's behavior as a direct result of an absent parent rather than as a result of his psychological make-up. Unquestionably, family situations exacerbate fixations, but the fixations themselves stem from psychological patterns.

---

[18]   This is in contrast to Boss Boys, among others, who usually carry anger against one or both divorced parents.

For example, if Steve was a Go With The Flow Boy, he would not morph into a wild discipline problem because of his father's absence. The situation might instead lead to greater disengagement from life's tensions. In Steve's case, his mom was ignoring the real challenge: Steve's psychological structure, not his current relationship with his Dad, needed to be addressed.

Steve's energized demeanor made him highly personable. His newest passion was motocross, having left behind past passions of skateboarding, Brazilian ju-jitsu, and the video game Grand Theft Auto. He spoke excitedly about each of these activities until it was time to get to work.

Steve was bored almost immediately when we started to work on his history term paper. We would stop and start as he would bring up subjects that popped in his mind. At first, I humored his need to avoid doing his work. I then asked him what would be more *fun:* getting this project done now and then going home to do whatever he wanted, or talking with me and then going home to do this project on his own. He buckled down as much as he could, but still remained fidgety and distracted.

Over the next few weeks, we went through different variations of the same themes that I had with Jake from the earlier case study. Gaining *fun* and *freedom* through doing work first and having fun later was the dominant motivational theme. Intensity was the main work theme. Guess The Test, study bursts, and active positive engagement were the primary tactics suggested.

Steve was neither as academic as Jake (the Adventure Boy in the introduction) nor as mature as the older Doug (the other Adventure Boy referenced earlier) so the change was slower going. But, his mom noticed his grades were improving, if not his way of being.

Then, we caught a break. Steve went to visit his father during February vacation. His stepmother's son from a prior marriage attended a university within driving distance. Steve's father thought it would be a good idea for Steve to spend a couple of days with his stepbrother to get a sense of college life.

When Steve returned, my commentary about the *fun* and *freedom* of college now had a tangible feel. It was neither the parties nor the girls that really shifted Steve. It was the feeling of being able to do what he wanted when he wanted to do it. "It was amazing. You could just walk out of your dorm and do a thousand different things."

After we discussed many of the fun options that would be available to Steve, I asked him about his willingness to do the work needed to gain admission to college. "It would be totally worth it," he exclaimed.

At the time of our initial interaction, Steve only had a rough idea of what he would do after high school, but he had resigned himself to thinking he would either attend the local community college or commute to a nearby small state school. He now had a vision in place for his post high school escape.

I had Steve put a picture on the desk that he used for studying of him and his stepbrother having fun in college. Every time he started to drift away, I wanted him to take a look at the picture.

Steve's big picture vision was now in place. On a day to day level, Steve was only a slightly better version of his past self, but from a technical study skills level, he was willing to embrace the intensity of Guess The Test. His grades shifted dramatically upward. While he never became a disciplined homework machine, he did understand that doing well on big tests was the best way he could change his grades. For that reason, he really put a great deal of energy into active studying for tests. He also really understood that it was boring to study large amounts of material in a passive way, and that while *fun* might not be the exact word to describe self-testing, at least he found it intense. He became very good at predicting and taking tests. It was a challenge. While it would never compete with motocross and he would never quite admit the following, I think he actually enjoyed himself a bit when he was engaged in self-testing.

In addition, after explaining (and re-explaining!) how being an "active-negative" really hurt his class participation grades, Steve picked his spots far better for his antics. While he did get into some trouble during study halls and lunches, he actually was viewed by a couple of his teachers as an asset in class because he would participate and raise the energy of the class.

Steve's story had a great ending. He wound up at the college with his step-brother and near his father. This helped him further develop a good relationship with his father. In addition, his newly found ability to do well on big tests was perfect for college where grades are almost exclusively related to big tests such as mid-terms and finals.

Action Steps

Earlier in the book, Jake's story was that of an Adventure Boy. Many of the action steps needed for Adventure Boys were presented in his case study.

While it could be said that Go With The Flow Boys are most in need of gaining intensity, Adventure Boys are most in need of having their natural intensity channeled in productive directions. Enhancing their studying intensity is important and tactics such as study bursts work well. More importantly, they need a big picture vision that stems from their personal beliefs. They are natural rebels and freedom seekers. Telling them to comport with your vision won't help. But if you get them excited about their vision, they will fly.

Chapter Nine

Star Boys

Who is my audience?

Brief Description

If your son likes to "perform" (whether literally in a public arena or figuratively to the crowd), does so in a conventional way (unlike Dreamer Boys who like to perform in unconventional ways), could be at once persuasive-charming and manipulative-deceitful, and is highly focused on projecting the right image, then your son is probably a Star Boy. Star Boys are concerned with their appearance, how they come across to others, and how to cultivate a public image.

Star Boys like to stand out. Striving to get positive attention for worthwhile achievements is the upside. When Star Boys feel that doing well in school is part of their image, they will work as hard as any student. But when the drive to perform is for the wrong crowd, trouble is inevitable.

Psychological Profile

To understand how a Star Boy will perform ask: "Who is the audience?" If in a peer group that really values academics, then academics will not be an issue. However, not many teen-boy peer groups fall into that category.

What teen boy doesn't want public approval? True. But Star Boys are more fixated on outward success than others, and therefore need applause to validate their image. On the issue of image orientation, the inner battle between the inauthentic façade and the authentic person is often the root of their challenges.

Immature Star Boys do not really know what they want. Rather, they want what they think others value. The invisible "they" is particularly significant to Star Boys as in "what will *they* think?" If asked, "Who are you trying to impress?" they don't really know, but everyone who matters to them is a fair answer.

The Challenges

Peer approval for high school boys stems primarily from athletics and popularity. Many Star Boys seek attention through sports and socializing with their friends. Subsequently, their school work suffers.

Further, where doing well in school is mocked, Star Boys might engage in self-sabotage, purposely not doing well in order to fit in with the crowd. Even more likely, Star Boys will become class clowns or troublemakers if that is a way to score points with their buddies.

Star Boys might also come across as charming yet deceitful. Whether the deceit is to cover their tracks when they are doing something they should not be doing, or exaggerating tales of their success and lying about their failures, the growth for the Star Boy comes from a drive to be authentic.

The good news is that Star Boys might be the least likely of the types to get addicted to drugs[19] or get into serious trouble that will derail outward success. The bad news is that they are addicted to approval, and if their non-academic peers become the dominant audience (as seems to be nearly inevitable during adolescence), it will be a tough battle to redirect their considerable energy toward scholastic success.

The Hope

When Star Boys seek public approval for academic success, life for parents is quite good! They are self-directed. No need to nag. Due in part to the compulsion to reach their goals, Star Boys, if properly directed, are among the most naturally hard-working types. While they will certainly take any reward given, the accomplishment itself will be reward enough. If they have a specific goal such as a top tier college, or if they embrace their image as academically gifted, they will adapt a laser focus and high drive toward accomplishment.

In addition, Star Boys are one of the easiest to direct toward striving for conventional success because that image fits perfectly with their psychological fixation. Indeed, when I work with mature Star Boys, the discussions are almost always on "how to succeed" rather than why they should succeed. Indeed, igniting the intensity of Star Boys is not that hard. They are naturally strivers. The hope is that you can move their striving in a positive direction.

---

[19]   This comment is largely based on observation. But I also analyze the situation as follows: Star Boys are fixated on gaining public approval. Drug addiction, in most every crowd, represents failure. This is definitely not to say that Star Boys won't experiment. If they are with a crowd that does drugs, the likelihood that they, too, will engage in whatever makes them look good is extremely likely. Yet Star Boys are usually more controlled in their indulgences than other types and likely would avoid private immersion. I would guess that among a drug using crowd, a Star Boy is more likely to be the big drug dealer than the big drug user.

Case Study

I met Nick when he was a high school freshman. This was great fortune as I am fairly certain that without early psychological redirection his story would have turned out differently.

Nick was a two sport star in freshman football and baseball. His peer group consisted of athletes and those who admired athletes. They reinforced Nick's focus on sports to gain public approval.

To be clear, excellence in anything is important. Mastery of a sport requires the exact same dedication as mastery in academics. I love working with serious athletes because they understand the discipline and rigor needed to excel in any area.

Yet, as was the case with Nick, many young athletes hold delusions of grandeur about their own abilities. Athletic recruiting can be an extraordinarily helpful way to gain admission to college, but suburban athletes need to understand reality regarding their competition. Athletes from affluent suburbs do quite well nationally in sports such as crew, swimming, tennis, golf, and squash. These are sports where their comparative wealth provides access to pools, courts, and expensive equipment. There are also some sports where suburban athletes succeed like hockey and lacrosse, which combine the same economic dynamic with reduced competition due to the regional nature of each.

Sports such as football, basketball, and baseball do not provide such advantages. For example, when football players from our area in shoreline Connecticut vie for spots at Division I powerhouses, they do not fare well.

This was the case with Nick who simply was too small to play college football and whose baseball skills could, at best, present him the opportunity to make a Division III team as a walk-on. So, like most all others, academics would be his primary way to gain admission to college.

Nick's current academic performance would limit his possibilities. Fortunately, Nick was naturally very smart. He had done very well in elementary school and on statewide mastery tests. But in his middle school, where the populations of a couple of elementary schools converged, he set out to make his mark socially and athletically. His mom noted that Nick embraced the all too typical middle school boy paradigm that doing well in school would make others think he was nerdy. In an effort to impress, Nick began clowning around in class. Worse, from his mom's perspective, he would sometimes act like he was less intelligent than he was to take on the inauthentic persona of a "dumb jock."

The root problem was that Nick did not view academic success as a means of gaining public approval. So he turned into an overachiever in sports and an underachiever in academics. In addition, if one could be viewed as an achiever socially, then Nick was doing well in that area also. He had directed a great deal of energy to becoming popular and seemed to have hit his mark.

Nonetheless, working with Nick was very easy as he was eager to make a good impression. He was happy to discuss his *successes.* As he relayed his stories, it seemed that, inadvertently, his parents had fed the public approval monster. They made a big deal of his *success* on the football field and on the baseball diamond. In addition, his mom would tell her friends, in front of Nick, about all the girls who liked him and about his never-ending social life. As the adults nodded approvingly and smiled at his social status, Nick seemed to embrace his image as an athletic playboy.

Nick needed to understand the shifting nature of how "success" is viewed. I asked Nick what would be considered *success* at the end of high school.

"Getting into a good college."

What would be *success* after college? While it was not my place to judge Nick's dominant focus on equating *success* with "getting rich," I was happy that he understood that the likelihood of getting rich increased from academic rather than athletic training.

I asked Nick about some of his cousins whom his mom told me he admired. One of his cousins attended Amherst and the other Cornell. Relatives in his extended family fawned over them. I asked Nick why and he responded, "They are *successful*." Again, we discussed the changing nature of what *success* means at 15 compared to what it will mean at 18. Nick seemed to be shifting his motivational nature right before my eyes. He noted that he didn't want to be considered "a loser" if he went to a "bad school."

Nick and I then looked at his report card which averaged to a B minus.

"What kind of grades do I need to get into a good school?" Nick asked.

That was all I needed. I had him. We spent the next several sessions blending in a combination of what technically needed to change in his study habits to do well and imprinting an image of complete *success* for Nick to embrace.

I suggested that at the moment Nick was playing out a stereotypical image of a popular, good athlete who peaks in high school and then is considered less *successful* when academics become a more important part of the public perception of *success*. We discussed the complete package of what he might consider high school *success*; a balance of top academics, well developed activities, and a healthy social life.

Like all teens, Nick had his ups and downs, but more than other types, when Star Boys are properly motivated, they take off. And Nick did. His progress was stunning to others. His B-minus grades turned into high Bs and then the first As started appearing during sophomore year. Applause followed as he heard girls talking about how smart he was and as his parents celebrated his academic *success*. He relayed several stories about how others thought he was destined for *success*.

He still socialized and played sports at full throttle, but he was now disciplined in his studies and focused on making the most of his potential.

Nick now attends one of those "good schools."

Action Steps

1. **Switch the audience**
Star Boys have perhaps the greatest potential to dramatically shift their motivational energy. Since they are directed more by outer than inner approval, change of environment or alteration of their social group can have an immediate effect.

While switching schools is not a viable option for most families, discussing positive role models, successful family members, and older achievement-oriented students is one way to imprint a different audience.

2. **Modify peer influence**
Peer influence is particularly important for Star Boys as they are subconsciously playing to the crowd. For example, when Star Boys are put in new situations, they will quickly figure out what is desired by the group and then will act accordingly to gain approval of the group for those desired characteristics.[20] For this reason, having a peer group that either values academics or at least applauds your son's academic success is particularly vital for Star Boys.

3. **Create the post high school vision of success**
Whether you embrace the conventional view of success as admission to a good college or preparation for a prestigious

---

[20] When first thinking about the issue of Star Boys, I thought that this group should have no problems in school because academic success would be naturally attractive as part of the success package. In discussions with Dr. Hahn, I developed a better understanding. He pointed out that those with this personality type would strive to be the coolest biker if they were in motorcycle gang because that would be success within such a social framework.

career, realize that such a vision is powerfully compelling to most Star Boys. Helping Star Boys understand what post high school success means at an early age will help shift their energy.

Chapter Ten

Boss Boys

I'm in charge. Get out of my way.

Brief Description

If your son has the personality of a middle linebacker or you could picture him as a tough cop or in work where he is clearly in charge, then there is a reasonable chance that he is a Boss Boy. Boss Boys are one of the easiest patterns to identify. You will probably know if your son is a Boss Boy after simply reading this page. Energetically, you can feel their presence. They are dominant types. As an authority figure in their lives, it is nearly inevitable that you will experience a high degree of conflict with your Boss Boy son, or that at this point you have given up the small battles and only do battle over the meaningful.

Most teen boys have conflict with their parents, but the level of conflict is of a different dimension with Boss Boys. They are seemingly fearless in the face of threats, stubborn beyond reason, and – here's the reason for extended fighting – utterly comfortable in conflict. Boss Boys are usually louder, more aggressive, and more confrontational than others.

Boss Boys also project strength, confidence, decisiveness, and often humor. They are natural leaders. When directing their energy appropriately, they can make a dynamic and positive impact on whatever they are doing.

The Psychological Pattern

Boss Boys have power, dominance, and control as their primary motivational triggers. On the positive side, Boss Boys are decisive, protective, and direct. As would be expected, they seek leadership. This projection of strength conveys confidence. In many groups, Boss Boys are the alpha-male. The archetype of the intimidating yet lovable army general or football coach might come to mind as healthy Boss Boys all grown up.

The challenges for Boss Boys emanate from the flip side of those traits. Their decisiveness can lead to impulsiveness. Their protectiveness can lead to a fixation with winning battles, even over trivial issues. Their directness can manifest as insensitivity. Their desire to lead can make them toxic in groups which they do not control. The caricature of the school bully portrays the epitome of the down side of Boss Boys.

The Challenges

Within the context of school challenges, Boss Boys have a natural aversion to being dominated. For that reason, they often will have conflicts with teachers, particularly if they do not respect the teacher. Similarly, conflicts with authority figures such as school administrators and coaches are also likely.

If they are not motivated in school, they will do just enough work to suit their desire to control the situation. If they feel that doing their work gives them control – to avoid detention or extra assignments or getting punished or to earn rewards or (if you are really lucky) to gain admission to a school of their choice – then they will do their work. If they are unmotivated and do not mind the punishments meted out for poor grades, then screaming at or threatening them will have little effect.

Unless they have attained leadership in either their activities or a social group, Boss Boys often have a tough time during high school years. School is a structure that confines them, and then to varying degrees, they feel the same confinement at home. In each situation, they are not the boss. Outbursts are nearly inevitable as they confront the ordeal of being ordered around at the very time of life when they fully believe that they should be in control.

The Hope

The hope for Boss Boys is that they direct their desire to dominate in constructive ways. Helping them channel their aggressive energy toward becoming captains of sports teams, leaders of clubs, and positive leaders in the community is often the best approach for parents of Boss Boys.

In addition, mature Boss Boys can take care of themselves. This can really ease the emotional burden of parents who worry about how to best guide their child. With numerous Boss Boys who have made a positive upturn, I have said – and have had full agreement with their parents – "He knows what he is doing." That's a great relief for parents.

Indeed, when Boss Boys are on top of their game, they parent themselves. They forge their own path and do what's necessary to get there.

Case Study

I met Bobby at the end of 9th grade. His parents were divorced. His mom was intimidated by him. His dad had given up on him. Bobby was rowdy and abrasive. He was also funny, full of energy, and gregarious. In small doses he was great, but I did not envy his parents.

None of Bobby's grades were good, but his mom brought him to us based on the possibility that he would fail Spanish for the year. Bobby had caused his teacher fits by engaging in typical class clown behaviors. His teacher had thrown him out on several occasions. But the real challenge came when the Spanish teacher told Bobby that he had to do an extra assignment for causing disruption in class. The assignment would count as a full test grade. Bobby thought this was unfair and told his mom that he was not going to do the work. His mom was beside herself as a zero on the assignment would ensure an F for the course.

Boss Boys are wonderful when it comes to fighting for a cause they find worthy. They will stick up for weaker friends, challenge arbitrary decisions, and stay loyal to those on their team. The challenge with immature Boss Boys is that they have a hard time distinguishing between worthwhile and self-absorbed battles.

When Bobby's mom left us alone, I asked him why he thought the extra work was unfair. He explained that he understood why he should be punished for bad behavior and why he should lose points for classroom participation, but he did not understand why he should have to do extra work for joking around in class as "one thing had nothing to do with another." Bobby thought that the Spanish teacher never liked him and this was his way of "getting him."

I knew that Bobby was not going to be dissuaded. So, I simply asked him if not doing his work was the best way to *control* the situation. For a guy who was normally quick to respond, Bobby sat quietly to sort it out.

I told Bobby that I saw the extra homework assignment. It would take at most 30 minutes to complete. It wasn't the work that Bobby was fighting, but the fact that the Spanish teacher was trying to *control* him in an unfair manner. I explained, however, that his overall strategy had a flaw. Wasn't it the case that if Bobby didn't do his work he would be giving the Spanish teacher the ammunition he needed to fail him? In doing so, I pointed out that *he would lose the war* with his Spanish teacher.

Bobby couldn't help but curse out loud. He seemed to realize the dilemma he faced. He could either do the work which he viewed as unfair, or he could refuse to do the work and ultimately lose to his nemesis.

The theme of choosing his tactics, which sometimes would call for strategic retreat in order to win the big battle, became the theme of our shifting Bobby as he tried to figure out how to deal with school.

Bobby did do the Spanish assignment, but that was not a magical transformation moment. Bobby had his areas of strength, but he was not academically gifted. He really hated reading. That would prove to be the constant challenge as he made his way through English, history, biology, and essentially any subject that required a lot of reading. He also hated Spanish. This was one of the reasons he caused so much trouble in his Spanish class.

The big battle centered upon his college aspirations. His mom desperately wanted Bobby to attend. As she noted, since Bobby expressed no interest in the trades or in jobs that did not require a college degree, what else was he going to do? His dad did not want to spend the money, as he had concluded that Bobby would just waste the tuition.

As Bobby entered 11th grade, this issue became the primary drama in Bobby's family. Bobby had a lot of anger at his father over this and other issues. But, in his father's defense, at least in relation to college, Bobby had not displayed any evidence that he would make a reliable investment. With the divorce creating a burden on the family finances, Bobby's dad had a point: there was a reasonable chance that Bobby would fail out after a semester or two and thus waste thousands of dollars.

Bobby's battle with his dad became the leverage that was needed to motivate him. In the context of battle, Bobby performed at his best. While Bobby's mom lobbied on his behalf, she had no ammunition. How could she argue for Bobby given his grades in high school so far? Bobby's father was not an unreasonable man. He said that Bobby had to demonstrate evidence of decent grades before he would reconsider his decision.

With his father's blessing, I suggested to Bobby that he prove his father wrong; that he had full *control* over the situation and *could win the battle* if he chose. At the end of the meeting, I could tell that we had our hook. Bobby was not going to let his poor grades make him lose.

Bobby still had a long way to go with developing adequate study habits and dealing with subjects that demanded high reading comprehension ability. He did, however, comply more regularly, and when occasionally energized, would study intensely. He never received an A in an academic subject, but he did go from Cs and Ds to mostly low Bs, with a couple of Cs.

As a postscript, Bobby went on to study criminal justice in accords with his plan to become a police officer. When Boss Boys use their desire to protect in constructive ways, they can become great forces of good.

Action Points

1. Use of Judo: Leverage their need to control

The motivational paradigms that seem to work with Boss Boys are "power" or "dominance" or "control." Your job is to figure out the best judo moves to leverage the power of Boss Boys to guide them in a positive direction. Of all the types, they are the most likely to do the opposite of what you tell them just to show that they are in control. Unlike Adventure Boys — who will battle for freedom rather than power — Boss Boys need to feel like what they are doing stems from their decision.

2. Clear directives for rewards and punishments

Unlike other types that might have a challenge figuring out what they want, Boss Boys do know what they want, at least in the present moment. Rewards for good school work are certainly effective across the board as behaviorism does work in the short run for most, and Boss Boys are the most likely to respond effectively to rewards. Here's why: Social Boys will be happy with a tangible reward, but their real reward is their better relationship with their parents. Star Boys will be rewarded by the accomplishment in and of itself. Dreamer Boys will feel special or will simply enjoy being treated as special. Go With The Flow Boys will be happy with the peace resulting from their good grades, and Adventure Boys will be happy with more freedom. Boss Boys like the knowledge that they are in control of the outcome, and as such, taking action in order to control the receipt of a tangible award works particularly well for them.

3. Lose battles in areas of small consequence

With worry that this advice will seem cliché, choosing your battles is particularly important if you are a parent of a Boss Boy. Let them push the envelope a bit. Give them control on some issues that might irritate you but do not fundamentally affect your values. If you want them more involved in the family, give them the reigns – let them control family night. To leverage their desire to feel in control in relation to their school work, let them create their own work structure, get them to promise to keep their word about keeping the structure – as Boss Boys tend to be black and white thinkers – and then remind them when they break their word (which they will!).

Chapter Eleven

Dreamer Boys

I am not just special. I am unique.

Brief Description

If your son likes to be different, has his own individual style, places a particular value on being special, and could be viewed as particularly moody or has bouts of extended melancholy, then he is quite possibly a Dreamer Boy.

Dreamer Boys are often sensitive, caring sorts with impractical visions. They think and act differently than the majority. Those who are more expressive will also dress with a unique flair. Often quite bright in big picture creative ways, creative Dreamer Boys often have trouble with the day to day grind and other mundane aspects of school.

The Psychological Pattern

Dreamer Boys are romantics. Their future dreams feature them becoming not only special, but uniquely special. They often have the paradoxical inner world of the insecure egomaniac. At one level, they feel inferior, longing for something they feel they do not have, and a sense that they are misunderstood by society. Simultaneously, they feel superior to what they perceive as typical drones and think that they are misunderstood because they are more talented/creative/intelligent than others.

When feeling comfortable with their unconventionality, Dreamer Boys create their own unique path. When feeling misunderstood, Dreamer Boys both scorn and envy the conventionally successful.

The Challenges

Dreamer Boys can face major motivational problems when their rejection of conventionality is wholesale. While their drive for authenticity can be admirable, they can reject too much of the world as it is and view school as just another place where they are misunderstood.

In addition, due in part to feeling misunderstood by others, they often have an artificially negative attitude toward conventional success. This can lead to an antagonistic view against typical school-to-college career paths. For example, Dreamer Boys will claim that they do not care about going to a name brand school or having a career that leads to a lot of money. But for the less emotionally developed Dreamer Boy, this leads to a false front. They claim that everyone else is phony but Dreamer Boys often want the same things as others such as being popular or attending a good college or having a lot of money. So, their attempt to be genuine is undercut by their false claims that they "don't care" about such things.

The socialization of Dreamer Boys can also be an issue. Introverted Dreamer Boys face the challenge of being misunderstood and lonely. As such, they sometimes might be turned off by school entirely since it is a painful social experience. Having at least one good friend in school will go a long way to help them avoid hating school. More extroverted Dreamer Boys will draw attention to themselves through dressing or acting unconventionally. This may lead others to ridicule them for their differences, but secure Dreamer Boys are willing to pay that price as they are proud of being unique. Dreamer Boys are more likely to join groups where their differences are appreciated. While this will seem stereotypical, a high percentage of Dreamer Boys are involved in theatre and music.

More than other types, Dreamer Boys face the problem of having to shift from a fixed to a growth mindset. Those with a fixed mindset believe that they naturally have certain strengths and weaknesses, and will forever flourish in areas of strength and flounder in areas of challenge. Those with a growth mindset believe that they can develop their skills and implicitly understand that there will be periods of trial and error as they build their abilities.

When not properly motivated, Dreamer Boys will believe that their natural strengths (their "specialness") will win out regardless of their work ethic. If, for example, they think they are innately capable in a subject area, they will feel comfortable "winging it." This usually works out well enough in K-8 when studying is not as critical, but challenges emerge thereafter when the level of difficulty requires study.

Dreamer Boys will often avoid striving in areas of weakness (those that have nothing to do with their specialness), and instead dismiss those areas as non-consequential. If, for example, they are not particularly strong in math, they are highly likely to avoid grinding out a good grade, and are more likely to simply view math as irrelevant to their dreams.

The Hope

As feeling types, Dreamer Boys, when not in a self-absorbed mode, are often very sweet-natured. In addition, their future visions and unusual way of looking at things almost always make them interesting.

In relation to the paradoxical quality of Dreamer Boys, their often overt appearance of insecurity may mask their internal view that they think of themselves as special (and many, in fact, are special!). This attribute often spurs Dreamer Boys to go after their big dreams. They do not see themselves sitting in office cubicles or being a face in the crowd at a college football game. They can see themselves doing something grand. And, for that reason alone, true greatness is possible. Many successful men who have designed unique companies, products, or services — or who did take the risk of following an artistic path — started out as Dreamer Boys. When Dreamer Boys are patient enough to deal with the length of time between the present reality and the future actualization of their dreams, and willing enough to deal with rigors required to get there, they quite often make their dreams come true.

Case Study

Kenny's parents called with great worry. Kenny had been a straight-A student through middle school. His writing was first rate. He was also a talented musician, but they worried that his interest in music had begun to take precedence over his school work.

Kenny's grades had slipped in 9th grade. He was having trouble with the volume of homework in high school and would occasionally skip assignments or turn in shoddy work. Kenny's grades stayed strong in English and history, but his math and science grades had dipped into the low B range. The decline continued in the first quarter of his sophomore year. His Algebra II grade caused the most worry as it was the first C he had ever received. But the rest of his grades, B- in Chemistry, B in French, B+ in History, and A- in English were lower across the board as well.

Kenny's parents were most concerned that Kenny had recently responded "musician" when a relative asked about his career aspirations. They expressed that he did not understand reality and was blowing his college chances by focusing on his new passion for writing songs.

I met Kenny when he was in the second quarter of his 10th grade. While he was not exactly dressed in gothic style, his outfit seemed to shout "I'm different." Since I dress professionally, which I know creates an oft-putting conventional aura to such teenagers, Kenny was initially quite withdrawn.

As soon as I said, "You seem more interesting than most students your age," Kenny made eye contact. "It must be tough to interact with some of the boys in your grade," I went on, as I gathered that Kenny did not particularly fit in well with the typical high school pack. Kenny nodded.

"You are going to love college because that's when guys who think deeply are appreciated more." Kenny was now paying careful attention to what I was going to say next.

"But we have to make sure that we figure out the right college for you because the normal, standard variety school might not suit you. We need some place that will help cultivate what makes you *special*."

In terms of what they want to study, "music" and other romantic yet atypical career paths are often the focus. Dreamer Boys, by the way, would not want to discover that they fit any cliché.

I do need to provide some commentary on the arts before I continue. I am not interested in bursting the bubble of would-be artists, musicians, or those headed toward a non-traditional career path. I left the legal profession to become an education-entrepreneur, which, while not anywhere near as dreamy as a musician, was viewed by most as a highly impractical decision.

I do know, however, that many of our young clients dream their dreams while living a comfortable lifestyle provided for them by their parents. Most have not had sufficient financial education to understand what it takes for their parents to provide such a lifestyle. Their attachment to their dreams is really only tested when they are asked to sacrifice.

I asked Kenny about his career dreams. He responded: "I know you are going to think it's stupid, but I want to be a musician."

I assured him that I didn't think it was a bad idea and pulled my ace card. I know Damien Kulash, the lead singer of OK Go (Even many parents have seen the dancing on a treadmill video, among others, that has helped make OK Go a big music success and an Internet sensation.) I know Damien through his sister, Trish Sie, who was the choreographer of those world famous videos, and is now hugely successful in her own right. That they are Ivy-league graduates (Damien from Brown and Trish from Penn) is one of the best parts of their story. They, too, had come from a similar background as Kenny, but I vividly remember Trish saying that they would live out of their car if they had to in order to pursue their rock star dreams. In addition, they had a great Plan B in place, as they both had first rate educations.

I asked Kenny how committed he was to his vision. He thought quite committed. I suggested that we come up with a plan. Artists need to be discovered. I pointed out that our idyllic shoreline community in Connecticut is a wonderful place to grow up, but no place for a serious musician to gain any publicity. After high school, he ought to move to New York. Kenny liked the idea because that's where he wanted to move.

I noted that he would need money and suggested that he could get a job waiting tables while he practiced his craft. "How many hours would I have to work?" he asked. I explained that New York is quite expensive. He would likely need to get a roommate or two through classified ads, and that a full 40-hour work week waiting tables or something similar was needed. "But you'll get to pursue your dream of becoming a musician," I said, knowing full well that Kenny's commitment to becoming an artist was now being tested.

Kenny asked about the apartments in New York. My office is about 700 square feet. I noted that his entire apartment would likely be half that size and that he would need to share that space with at least one roommate. Having come from reasonable affluence, Kenny's face seemed to distort.

I emphasized again that he would be able to develop his music when he was not waiting tables. I knew that the romantic notion of his vision was beginning to fade. "Maybe I could go to college like the OK Go guy?" Kenny suggested. Yes, I noted. Damien and Trish had cultivated their artistic abilities while simultaneously building their conventional credentials. Maybe that path made sense . . .

The goal from an academic coach's perspective is to leverage the vision of Dreamer Boys. By helping Dreamer Boys understand that by doing better in school they are more likely to be able to chart their paths to their dreams, Dreamer Boys become more willing to deal with the tedium of school.

Kenny set his sights on New York University. NYU has a long, storied history of producing actors, but there is also an impressive list of musicians who attended NYU: Neil Diamond, for old-timers, Albert Hammond of The Strokes for those under 30, and also a certain Stephanie Germanotta, better known as "Lady Gaga".[21]

NYU also requires top grades. Kenny was intellectually capable of getting high marks, but lost significant points per quarter due to his homework habits. Dreamer Boys have a hard time with routine tasks. Dealing effectively with the mundane is the Achilles Hill of many Dreamer Boys. In Kenny's case, although he was now more motivated due to his vision, he still had to deal with the day to day grind of school.

Kenny's mom noted that quite often he would take out his homework, but would not start as he seemed to be lost in his thoughts. I suggested that when possible she chat with him about what was his on his mind, soothe his emotional bumps,

---

[21] She dropped out before graduation, but I think it worked out for her.

and then ease him into his work. That seemed to help a great deal in getting him started.

Kenny's issue with school was certainly not intelligence. He dedicated himself to gaining admission to NYU. He was a brilliant writer and gained not only As in English but also the English prize at his prep school. While never great in math and science, he managed to do enough to get B pluses. He isn't done with high school yet, but whether or not he gains admission to the college of his dreams is almost immaterial. He has developed his work character. He is on his way to building his dreams.

Action Steps

1. Channel the Dreamer Boy's emotional energy

Dreamer Boys have a far harder time than most other boys in compartmentalizing their feeling state. For example, motivated Star Boys may be dealing with a big emotional issue, but will invariably do what is necessary to get their work done. Not so with Dreamer Boys whose bad moods or sadness will interfere with productivity. When I work with students of this type, I allow them to vent for a bit if it seems that this will help get them started. You should also understand that their emotional state will affect their productivity. When moody or melancholic, Dreamer Boys may simply need to process their inner states. Feeling connected or understood is important. Having non-judgmental conversations with Dreamer Boys about their feelings is helpful.

2. Let them have some creative control over their work structure, but ensure that their busy work is completed with quality.

While not aggressive in their rebellion, Dreamer Boys tend to revolt against structure. They like the feeling of doing things with their own unique imprint. For more forceful types, such as Adventure Boys and Star Boys, the intensity of structure can work well. Dreamer Boys may rebel against structure for the sake of creating their own unique way of work. It will be helpful to allow some creative control over their work style while mandating that results must be produced.

3. Show them both the practical steps and challenges related to their impractical dreams

You may be tempted to dissuade them about impractical paths. However, you will succeed more if you show them the challenges rather than telling them that you think their path does not make sense. That the path does not make sense to normal people is part of the appeal to Dreamer Boys.

If you want to encourage their dreams, leverage their desire to be special. Play into the vision by showing them the practical steps that will help them get where they want to go. When I give presentations on career paths, I often note that artistic types are in the most need of financial education. I mean this sentiment not to dissuade would-be artists, but rather to help enable them to become financially savvy enough to manage their bills while they pursue their dreams.

Chapter Twelve

Social Boys

I want to be liked.

Brief Description

If your son is in a constant state of hanging out with his friends and girlfriend, or perpetually texting or Facebooking (if that is now a verb), and needs — NEEDS — to be engaged with his friends as much as possible, then you probably have a Social Boy. While the need to be well liked and accepted may seem universal among high school boys, Social Boys have a particularly acute desire to be popular, or at least well liked within their crowd.

Social Boys, as one would guess, are relationship focused. Therefore, they are more prone to relationship drama than other guys. That drama is usually focused on their girlfriend or hoped-for girlfriend, because most guys will not tolerate such neediness.

Social Boys are more loving and affectionate than other teen boys. As a parent, this is a huge plus. They typically want to enter people professions, particularly those focused upon helping others.

Psychological Profile

Social Boys want to be needed by others. Their normal state is approval seeking, but in a different way than Star Boys who want to be thought of as successful more than they want to be liked. Social Boys would choose friends/loved ones over achievement. They will adapt the stance of helper within a relationship. They will be the social coordinators of the group, the ones who buy the gifts and remember the birthdays, and the good friends who come through whenever needed.

The darker side of the Social Boy stems from his fixation with wanting others to need him. There can be a manipulative quality to his giving nature. Even if only at a subconscious level, he gives with the expectation of getting in return. Jealous, dramatic and needy, immature Social Boys can be overbearing. While a teen boy won't act in the same ways as the archetype of the guilt-inducing grandmother, the psychological profile is similar.

The Challenges

Social Boys care primarily about their relationships. Academics are often a distant second. Social distraction causes lack of focus in class, in studying, and in motivation. In class, Social Boys will not cause much trouble because they do like to please their teachers, but they almost can't help but chatter with their friends. During study time, any technological device that connects them with others will be used. As for motivation, their drive is more naturally directed toward people than books.

Almost always extroverted, Social Boys have a hard time engaging in solitary studying. While Social Boys are less dramatic than girls with the same psychological pattern, those who focus on relationships usually will end up with some interpersonal drama. Social Boys who have girlfriends or who are longing to have a girlfriend may immerse themselves in very distracting melodrama that hinders their academic success.

Social Boys typically do far better in classes where they connect with the teacher. When the teacher is distant and treats them merely as "student" rather than attempting to connect with them as individuals, they tend not to try as much.[22]

The Hope

Great news for parents: if your Social Boy develops emotionally, he will be an outstanding son who cares for you all your life. His very nature is focused on giving and pleasing. For this reason, Social Boys are often attuned to what pleases parents and willing to do what makes their parents happy.

On the academic front, if Social Boys have a sense that advancing academically will really help their relationships, including with their parents, they will do what is asked. Having a peer group that values academics is particularly important for Social Boys to succeed, since the desire to look good to the group is important to Social Boys.

Case Study

Every few minutes, Luke's phone would buzz with the urgency of yet another text. On weekends, he would beg his mom to have his friends stay over or ask if he could stay over at one of his buddies. He did not miss a social event or party, but he did miss his homework from time to time. Luke's mom had been sympathetic, as she had been a similar type of teen. But Luke's almost straight Cs – and a lone B in English with his favorite teacher – brought his mom to see us.

---

[22] I doubt many Social Boys become research scientists or enter other highly specialized professions that require solitary problem-solving. Their need to connect with people is usually too strong.

In addition, Luke's roller coaster emotional state (related to his girlfriend) started to affect the entire family. Luke's father is a good guy, but having grown up with three brothers who all focused on sports, and having spent the majority of his time in the world of finance, he simply could not relate to his son's high emotional needs. He had tuned Luke out and had become a distant father.

As a general motivational paradigm, those who are thinking-oriented can be persuaded by reason. Those who are feeling-oriented need their emotions shifted before acting. For the most part, Social Boys and Dreamer Boys are feeling-oriented. Luke's Dad was highly thinking-oriented and grew frustrated with efforts to motivate Luke through reason.

Unlike Dreamer Boys, who can be shifted by an emotionally powerful vision of potential work success, Social Boys are not primarily motivated by accomplishment in and of itself. This is not to say that they are not interested in achievement, but rather they are more interested if it will increase the likelihood that those they care about will care about such outward success. When Social Boys are young, they are concerned about pleasing their parents and thus motivating them to do well in school is easy. As peers become more influential, Social Boys become more focused on developing friendships, being socially connected, and becoming popular.

In relation to Luke, I met with his parents alone, as I needed to figure out how to get his parents – particularly his father—back as Luke's primary influencers.

Luke's Dad was noticeably uncomfortable when I presented the situation. He typically did his own thing on the weekend. Between golf in the warm weather and watching football in the cold weather, he had disconnected from Luke. He noted that Luke was not interested in his stuff and, quite frankly, he was not interested in Luke's stuff. He also had deferred to Luke's mom on issues related to Luke.

Initially defensive, Luke's Dad shifted when he poignantly recalled the days when Luke had been his "little buddy" and clamored for his attention. To his credit, his initial hesitation at dealing with the issue turned into a project that he embraced: reconnecting with his son. Luke's mother could relate perhaps too much to Luke. She had been a Social Girl. Her grades had suffered in high school. She did receive her associate's degree, but she always felt she could have done more and now was stuck in administrative job with no potential.

She also had not realized that in an effort to be Luke's friend, she was inadvertently feeding the emotional drama beast. For example, when Luke would get off the phone with his girlfriend, she would dissect the nuances of the conversation in a way that would convey to Luke that he had been involved in an important discussion. Further, she would find herself invested in the social drama that occasionally enveloped Luke's life. In doing so, she reinforced the significance of these issues. When I met with Luke, I directly addressed his relationship with his parents. He was tired of the nagging from his Dad about his school work. "That's all he ever talks to me about." I asked him how he thought his Dad felt when Luke did not try his best. "I guess he feels disappointed in me." Do you think your Dad might also feel disappointed in himself? I asked Luke.

Luke had not thought of the situation that way before. Feeling types are motivated when their emotional state is activated. Luke had never empathized with his father over this issue. I explained to Luke that his father was not just disappointed by Luke's performance, but that he was also disappointed in himself for not being able to help Luke.

I asked Luke what he thought was important. He said he knew what I would say: that I thought his interest in hanging out with his friends and girlfriend so much was "silly," as his Dad had told him.

I assured him that caring about his friends was a wonderful trait. That surprised him. I then asked him to consider the fact that he was soon moving to another world of people, and that his grades would be critical in his capacity to control which group of people would encompass his future friends.

I gave him a hypothetical: What if he were told that his current school would close down at the end of the year and he had to attend another local high school? And if he and all his friends could request which school they wanted, but with the following catch — only those at the top half of the class would get their first choice. Would that cause him to work harder? Yes, of course.

As I knew the social hook was the key, I suggested that college choice was similar. I brought up certain colleges that had distinct stereotypes of students who attended those colleges. Naturally, some of these groups appealed to Luke and others did not. I asked, "Do you want to control the choice of people you hang out with?"

I mentioned that I met my wife in college. Luke was very happy that there would be many women to meet in college.

I then asked Luke, "As you get older, do you think women are impressed by those who do well in school or those who are slackers?" Luke began speaking animatedly about the change that he was already beginning to see related to this issue. In middle school, girls did not care how anyone performed academically in school. But now, girls were talking about where the senior guys were going to college. "I guess college girls will be interested in my grades and what kind of job I'll have when I graduate."

As Luke left, he said, "No one ever talked to me about college like this before." And that was exactly what was needed to ignite him to care.

Luke visited a few colleges and realized that he felt much more socially comfortable at some schools than others. In conversations with Luke, it seemed that gaining admission to those schools was being processed as gaining admission to his preferred potential group of friends.

Some additional positive developments helped Luke's transition. His father began spending more time with him and I would guess that Luke's deeper connection to him inspired him to please his father with better grades. His mother deemphasized social drama and instead talked to Luke about her career. She had long desired to enter the health care field and was considering heading back to school to do so.

During the next few months, Luke developed an interest in becoming a physician assistant. At the time, it was not clear whether this was due to a subconscious desire to please his mother or a genuine interest in health care, but it was evident that he had a new found intensity toward school. Luke had dug his hole a bit too deep to recover and gain admission to his first choice colleges – those GPAs are cumulative – but several excellent results ensued through this work. Luke developed work character. From this point on in his life, Luke knew he could work and call upon his developing focus, willpower, and discipline to accomplish his goals. Luke had a defined career path. As expected, the health care field fit his desire to help others. While he was not certain if he would become a physician's assistant or a nurse practitioner, he knew the direction that interested him. Perhaps, most importantly, Luke and his Dad rebuilt their relationship.

Action Steps

1. Establish very clearly that you care about achievement

Modern parents worry too much about appearing like movie caricatures of the parents who only care about achievement. Too many parents will sacrifice their desire to be liked for the greater good of demanding that their children work hard to reach their potential. Social Boys, more than any other type, need clear direction that you care about grades. Of course, parents should communicate that they love their children regardless, but if you give such an opening to a Social Boy, without also giving the clear message "and I expect that you will do your best and I will be disappointed otherwise," you will give the Social Boy room to not strive.

2. Do whatever you can to ensure that he has at least one friend who cares about school

Peer groups matter to all, but more so to Social Boys and Star Boys. It is extremely hard to control friendships, but in whatever subtle ways possible, steer your Social Boy to friends who care about school.

3. Deemphasize relationship drama

This tends to be advice for Moms more than Dads. If your Social Boy is worried about his girlfriend, give him the following true advice: the only girl who will really matter to him is his future wife! No need to have drama over romance during the teen years.

4. Cut off social connectivity during study time

This is really a "nuts and bolts" piece of advice and one that could be applied to all students. The draw to chat is simply too enticing for Social Boys. No social connection during study time. None.

5. Encourage building of relationships with teachers

Social Boys need good relationships with their teachers in order to feel connected to their classes. There is an element of luck involved in having teachers that could bond with your son. Even so, encourage (or push) your son to better get to know those teachers with whom he does not naturally click. If the teacher offers after-school help, take advantage of such help even if only to allow for informal socialization between the teacher and your son.

PART IV

Chapter Thirteen

The Other Patterns

What about other patterns?

There are several answers. The most obvious: any theoretical personality construct that creates labels for humans will always fall short in boxing billions of people into a finite number of categories. The boxes, however, help us communicate concepts. The hope is that at least one of the patterns will be helpful in changing how you communicate with your son.

More importantly, I hope that the general concept of motivating your son through triggers related to his psychological profile will help you more effectively inspire him.

Those familiar with the Enneagram are no doubt wondering about the other three types in the system? Where are Points 1, 5, and 6? Students of each type have their academic challenges. But, as a generality, motivational issues related to academics are not their biggest challenge, at least as far as I can tell from my work with Points 1 and 5. I will explain the complicated issues with Point 6s who seem to be either doggedly motivated or extraordinarily rebellious. In addition, as noted earlier, I am not particularly interested in staying purely within the confines of the Enneagram.[23]

Nonetheless, here are some brief explorations of the three remaining Enneagram types.

---

[23] In addition, the Enneagram itself does not really confine personalities into 9 types. Within each of the nine types, there are three subtypes. And each type is influenced by the dominance of one of its wings; whether the person is in a secure or stressed state; and the person's level emotional development. So even within this confined system, there are hundreds of different ways to slice the pie.

Chapter Fourteen

Perfect Boys

I am not quite right.

Brief Description

Perfect Boys have an unusual set of problems that often go undetected because, at first glance, the challenges do not seem like problems at all. Rule-oriented, good kids, Perfect Boys try to do the right thing – with "usually" attached to the following descriptions: they do their homework, pay attention in school, and cause little trouble.

I meet Perfect Boys when parents call and describe their child "as a good kid, but one who procrastinates" . . . and then the parent qualifies the remark . . . "it's not that he doesn't sit down to do his work, but rather that he doesn't get things done in a timely way." They often add, "and he really struggles with big tests."

Psychological Pattern

Perfect Boys are self-critical by nature. They fall short of reaching their impossibly self-imposed high standards. Their internal dialogue can be deflating because it centers upon their shortcomings. And, with the loss of self-confidence, motivation to strive begins to ebb.

Perfect Boys pay particularly close attention to authority figures. Their inner world is often a magnification of parental programming. What you say to your Perfect Boy will be volume enhanced and played on repeat. Since their natural attraction is toward gaining perfection through overcoming their flaws, your criticisms will be heard loud and clear. Many parents of Perfect Boys tell me that they balance their criticisms with compliments, but Perfect Boys tune out the compliments and tune in the negative feedback.

The Challenges

Misdiagnosed procrastination is the most common reason we receive a call related to a Perfect Boy. When parents call to cite their concern about their student-child not finishing his work, I hear sympathy rather than exasperation.

Parents of other types will call and, with a fed-up tone, describe how their son wants to do nothing but hang out with his friends or play video games. On the other hand, Perfect Boys have been trying to do their work, but somehow have trouble getting it done. Parents usually have compassion for their child's plight and realize that their son has been inefficient, not unmotivated.

This inefficiency can lead to stress and exhaustion, both of which lead to lower levels of motivation.

Perfect Boys try to do things . . . perfectly. So when an assignment calls for them to read pages 181-217, they will do exactly as directed. In and of itself, that's not a problem. But due to time pressure, their style does not work effectively.

Efficient types will naturally focus on concepts that might be on a test – the bold words in the text – while the Perfect Boy may examine the full text with equal focus. In addition, some students intuitively understand that any extended reading assignment usually requires an understanding of the big picture and memorization of critical facts (those "bold terms") for the test. These efficient students might pay high attention to the areas that seem significant, yet scan through other areas that they guess are not as important. Perfect Boys, even if they consciously understand otherwise, have an internal sense that they should read every word with equal vigor and memorize as much as possible. They become overwhelmed. Burn-out is common. If they start to feel unmotivated to work, burn-out stemming from caring too much, rather too little, is the culprit.

Writing proves to be another area of challenge. Writer's block, common for many, is the norm for the Perfect Boy. As noted, parents will often lead with the not-quite-right description "he procrastinates" as they relay a story about "yet another paper that he is finishing at the last minute." But the Perfect Boy's procrastination is different than, for example, the Adventure Boy's fun-oriented procrastination. Perfect Boys are suffering while they are not getting things done.

Multiple choice testing, most significantly standardized testing, also causes great challenge. Educated guessing is the process by which most successful test-takers move forward. Perfect Boys will suffer over the possibility of getting something wrong. Time pressure, caused by their pondering, becomes a big issue. Perfect Boys will delay putting down an answer until they are sure they have it right. And that becomes a major issue when dealing with hard problems on standardized tests, which reward a more aggressive style.

Case Study

"He is up until midnight every night," Mike's mom started the conversation, "and he takes so much time when he tests that he underperforms."

I met Mike. He was wonderfully polite and attentive. Mike was easy to work with, as he was eager to please and willing to do what was asked. We began our work together with test preparation for the SAT. Mike was very bright, but he kept getting in the way of himself. He would take an inordinate amount of time on problems. He would second guess himself. He would suffer when he was wrong. He would comment that he was "stupid."

"Why don't you simply guess?" I asked Mike as he suffered through yet another problem. "I might get it wrong," he answered. While no one likes to be wrong, Perfect Boys hate to be wrong. They suffer over being wrong. And their suffering leads to classic cases of "analysis paralysis."

The manifestation of this problem showed up when he was completing assignments, writing papers, and taking tests. Over the last year, he had a done a good job of convincing himself that he was dumb because he could not work fast. Yet his psychological, not intellectual, processing speed was the problem. He simply could not move forward until he felt he had done something perfectly.

"The perfect is the enemy of the good." I made Mike repeat the statement several times. He understood the dictum that trying to be perfect undermined accomplishing good things, but in practice, he would still resist moving forward efficiently. Strange as it may sound, his challenge was overcoming the need be a good boy at all times.

Good boys do not consciously do things that might be wrong. "Guessing" is exactly that – doing an act that might be wrong.

We discussed aspects of his childhood and his desire to please his parents. His parents were not particularly different than other parents, at least compared to those in our client base who expect their children to work hard. But Mike had taken his parents' demands far more to heart than others. He really worried about disappointing them.

We began to discuss what would happen if he disappointed his parents. Mike seemed more emotional than I expected.

Mike had internalized their criticisms in a way that made him feel that any mistake was a failure of significant proportions.

This insight is vital for parents of Perfect Boys: they will magnify your criticisms, record those comments, and play them on an endless loop.

Some good results from having an internal critic: Perfect Boys rarely get into trouble. You can trust Perfect Boys when you are not looking. It is highly unlikely that they will do the reckless things that make parents stay up worrying at night.

They will not forget their mistakes, however, and this in part is what creates inefficiency in studying, procrastination in writing assignments, and indecisiveness on standardized multiple choice testing.

While there are certain techniques that work wonderfully well with helping Perfect Boys become more efficient (such as Guess The Test), the bigger challenge with Perfect Boys is helping them become kinder bosses to themselves.

I asked Mike to pretend he was the boss of a group of people. Would he treat others the way that he treated himself? He understood what I was saying, but retorted that he needed to be self-critical in order to get results. I asked him if he thought it was possible to get results without such self-criticism. He wasn't sure, but he was willing to find out.

Over the weeks that followed, Mike attempted to minimize his self-criticism. Like us all, his internal programming was too strong to immediately change, but he became aware of his pattern and awareness can make all the difference.

Mike's grades had generally been good, so his improvement was marginal. It was in standardized testing that his new mindset shifted him. Mike had a significant problem with reading comprehension on the SAT. Unlike math, where there is a definitively best answer or what could be called a "perfect" answer, correct reading answers are the "best choice." But the best choice is rarely a perfect answer and is often just the best answer among not particularly great choices.

Mike had really struggled with timing because he would look through the answers again and again in the hopes that he would know with certainty that he was answering correctly. His initial reading score was 480, a slightly less than average score, but surprisingly low for a student of his abilities.

Through extensive training, I forced Mike to make educated guesses, and tried to imprint that getting rid of incorrect answers was the "right thing to do." He flourished and wound up with a reading score in the high 600s.

More importantly, Mike was now aware that if he treated himself more kindly he could have both success and happiness.

Chapter Fifteen

Observer Boys

I want to be alone.

Brief Description

If you can picture your son immersed in a solitary activity involving his mind for the entire weekend, you probably have an Observer Boy.

Shy, withdrawn, and bookish, we do not have many Observer Boys come to us for academic motivation issues. They are not necessarily the most intelligent of the types (although they might be!), but they are fixated with the life of the mind and therefore develop themselves intellectually more than others. They crave knowledge. If liberal arts oriented, they are big readers. If math oriented, they find challenging math problems fun.

Many future engineers, researchers, and scholars started as Observer Boys.

The Psychological Pattern

The world of the mind is where Observer Boys live. The outer world is often intrusive. Observer Boys have the personality type that is most suited to intellectual endeavors. For that reason, academic motivation is almost always not a problem unless their inherent desire for knowledge becomes directed toward fantasy (as in role-playing video games) or areas of interest that might be productive (computers) yet take away too much time from school.

The easiest way to spot an Observer Boy is to notice who in a crowded room isn't talking. Some Observer Boys are shy, as in not confident in speaking to others, but many simply prefer the solitude of their own mind over small talk. In fact, Observer Boys are often quite confident, particularly within areas that they consider themselves experts.

The Challenges

So what's the main school problem for Observer Boys? Usually, their challenges relate to energy and intensity to do anything outside of their intellectual interests. Many Observer Boys have great grades and test scores, but few activities. With the exception of long distance running, Observer Boys are usually not interested in sports. The remaining litany of high school clubs does not normally strike Observer Boys as particularly enlightening. You won't find many Observer Boys on Student Council.

There are some academic challenges related to school. Detached and aloof, Observer Boys often lose points for classroom participation, and to the extent that they do not build relationships with teachers, might also fail to get noticed. Public speaking assignments usually cause problems for the more socially awkward and shy Observer Boys.

Other issues are social. High school social life, filled with frivolity and kind to big extroverts, is not the best situation for the more serious-minded, introverted Observer Boys. If you are a social mom, you likely have some struggles connecting with your introverted son. But you also will be reasonably worry-free, as your Observer Boy is unlikely to get into much trouble. Further, one good friend is often all he needs socially, as he has a best friend already – his mind.

The Hope

Bill Gates. At least within Enneagram circles, the richest man in the world is thought to be of this type. Observer Boys have the capacity to concentrate on something of interest for hours and hours. Engineers, scientists, professors, computer programmers, and doctors (among other thinking professions) have always been well-suited possibilities for grown up Observer Boys. And now, the business world has also shifted further in their favor.

Just a generation ago, the ability to play office politics and navigate business-social arenas would provide significant obstacles for Observer Boys in the normal corporate world. The Information Age has opened up a plethora of possibilities for both creating wealth and earning a living without having to be an extrovert. A disproportionate number of those multi-millionaire tech wizards you read about were probably Observer Boys.

Case Study

"Josh is very smart, but he's not involved in any activities. I don't think colleges will like that, but he disagrees." Josh's mom was correct on that point. Despite the fact that Josh's grades and test scores were top notch, his lack of activities would hurt him in his quest to get into a top university.

My first meeting with Josh was tough. He had no interest in creating a personal connection. He did not make eye contact, volunteered no information about himself, and stuck to the bare-boned facts when answering questions.

Our "conversation" was so uninteresting that there is no dialogue that I can remember.

But he did listen.

Josh's mom called me, ecstatic after the meeting. "You really got through to him!" I was puzzled.

After coming home from our meeting, Josh went to his room and came out two hours later with a three-page bullet point document that he presented to his mom. It was an elaborate plan to start and develop a Manga Club that would span over multiple schools in our region, employ social media to develop, and involve forging relationships with Japanese high schools. Not surprisingly, most of the work could be done via technology and did not require meeting in person. Fortunately, Josh's mom was able to explain to me that Manga was a style of Japanese comics that Josh passionately enjoyed.

What happened in the meeting that I didn't see? I walked Josh through a logical presentation of the need for depth in activities to distinguish him from all the other top students who were applying to the same level of schools. I noted that every high school in America has students who have outstanding grades, and that many of those students also had top test scores. I explained how he needed to differentiate himself to stand out among similarly impressive students.

I then told Josh that if he couldn't find an activity that suited him, then he could create his own club. I provided several examples of how this could be done. He nodded, but gave me no indication that he planned on doing so. He was processing in a way that I did not fully understand.

That often is the case with Observer Boys who relate in eccentric and non-communicative manners. Dreamer Boys are equally unusual, but Dreamer Boys are highly communicative about their passions if they feel comfortable enough to share. While willing to talk about their areas of expertise for hours (think college professor!), Observer Boys do not feel the need to share with those who do not have similar interests.

The best suggestion for parents of Observer Boys: help cultivate a defined area of excellence toward a career path that will enable them to use that well-developed mind.

Chapter Sixteen

Worry Boys

What's the worst that can happen? I'll tell you.

Brief Description

Worry Boys are naturally anxious. They are averse to new things, situations, and people. If you find that your son *strongly objects* to trying new things, instinctively points out bad potential outcomes, and views disaster as just around the corner, he's probably a Worry Boy. Skeptical, questioning, and used to playing Devil's Advocate, Worry Boys will often appear argumentative.

Conversely, Worry Boys can be warm, loyal, dutiful, often funny, and make great friends (and sons) to those who have passed their initial guard. They also can be extremely hard working. Upon finding their group or cause, they are dedicated and committed troopers.

Worry Boys are the most complicated of all types. This is due to the Enneagram's framework which divides this personality type into phobic and counter-phobic variations. For sake of simplicity, I will direct this discussion toward the more easily understood phobic type.[24]

Psychological Pattern

The world, people, life, anything . . . are not automatically trusted by the Worry Boy. While fear of definite known dangers is part of the pattern, the bigger challenge is a pervasive state of anxiety toward the unknown. This core demon haunts Worry Boys until they discover a foundation through either group affiliation (be it familial, religious, cultural, or team) or a psychological-spiritual philosophy of life that shifts their existential distrust to dutiful faithfulness of a group or a cause.

Challenges

In relation to productivity, anxiety can be crippling. Fortunately, unlike Perfect Boys who may freeze due to anxiety, Worry Boys might just do the opposite. They will be amped-up, causing them to work and work and work. They just do so while feeling angst.

Worry Boys are often unwittingly aggressive in their questioning and thus oft-putting to teachers. Their challenging attitude might be misperceived as surliness, when in actuality, it might simply stem from intellectual curiosity. Learning how to deal with "office politics," even in a school setting, will be one of the constant challenges facing Worry Boys.

---

[24] If your son is a counter-phobic Worry Boy (Point 6 on the Enneagram), my sympathies are with you! Instead of following authority as phobic types do, they will automatically take a defiant stand against whatever they find threatening. And you, as the parent, are often the controlling authority that is threatening. To make matters more complicated, they do not appear overtly anxious, but rather present like Boss Boys with an aggressive, anti-authoritarian attitude. The difference is that Boss Boys not only do not want to be controlled, but want to control others. Counter-phobic Worry Boys want to avoid buying into anything that doesn't suit their individual code.

Hope

If they develop a value system that provides the proper character, Worry Boys can be both very warm – with those they love – and highly dutiful in caring out good works. And they often have great comic sensibility! Worry Boys might very well be the funniest of the types, in part because of their skewed way of articulating the absurdities in the world, their self-deprecating style, and their ability to pop the balloons of the inauthentic. David Letterman, among other comics, is usually thought of as an example of an Enneagram Point 6, a Worry Boy grown-up.

Further, the phobia that can paralyze Worry Boys from moving forward to try new things will also prevent them from trying harmful things and putting themselves in dangerous situations.

More good news: based on my observations, Worry Boys will work harder than any other type in school if they care about academics. By combining the intellectual drive of the Observer Boy with the workaholic nature of the Perfect Boy, Worry Boys will channel their anxiety toward academic achievement.

Case Study

John had done very well in school. His challenge was that he had recently taken the attitude that "everything was BS" according to his mom. This was beginning to affect his motivation, which resulted in what his mom was concerned would be a downward trend.

"What does it matter?" John asked. "I'm killing myself for nothing." While not articulating it as such, John was referring to his perpetually anxious state coupled with his sense that he was not exactly sure why he was working so hard without clear rewards.

We were in the teeth of The Great Recession and John's father had just been let go from a company that he had worked for over 20 years. John's father had been a top student, attained his doctorate in chemistry, and had been a dedicated, hard worker for a Fortune 500 company. His lay-off demonstrated to John that the world was not fair.

Fortunately, John's anxiety saved him from truly slacking. He seemed incapable of not doing his homework and not studying for tests. But his usual vigor was declining. Getting Bs did not seem like such a bad thing anymore. Maybe it wasn't, but he was capable of As. I told him so and he agreed.

John was a true intellectual, so we discussed his psychological challenges very directly. He understood in an advanced teen sort of way that his lack of external direction was stemming from his lack of internal foundation.

"What's the point?" was John's general question. Even if you studied hard, gained admission to a good college, and worked hard for a company, you could still get burned like his father. John had no spiritual base, either, but he was searching for something to trust.

"What about reaching your human potential?" I asked. This led to an interesting discussion about spirituality/agnosticism/ meaning of life and all those big questions that less-developed young adults don't consider until college.

John ultimately agreed that whether or not there was something more than biological determinism, he was "here" and maybe the whole point of being here was to do his best. And so he did. He reignited his intensity and resumed his march toward graduating near the top of his class.

Chapter Seventeen

Conclusion

Parents are the true heroes of education. This is not a slight to teachers, many of whom are equally heroic. But over time, I have observed the following: almost every student who had high-level work character had at least one parent who was a dominant force in shaping his motivational mindset.

The challenge for parents is that they have to straddle the roles of unconditional love giver with that of demanding boss. Both roles are necessary, but it makes motivating one's own child that much harder. The hope is that this book provides some helpful framework that will become part of your motivational arsenal.

The time could not be more momentous. The barriers to create an optimal work life at a young age have been largely removed. Talented, credentialed, go-getting young men with work character now have the capacity to design their own careers. With some good luck, many of these young men will be able to create happy and prosperous work lives far earlier than their counterparts of any prior generation.

Simultaneously, the world economy is more precariously perched than at any time since the Great Depression. I would rather create hope than despair. But clearly, many in the next generation will struggle if they do not develop their skills, credentials, and work character.

So what to do? In addition to taking greater control of your son's education, you need to inspire your son. And to do so, it would be helpful to have an understanding of your son's psychological blueprint. While we are all different, there are certain patterns of human behavior that recur. Some personality profiling tests provide data that can be useful in discerning the pattern of your son. Upon understanding your son's motivational triggers, you will be in a position to help shift him from being outer- to self-directed.

And if you do that, you will have done your job as parent exceedingly well.

Appendix A

A few data points on male underachievement

High school:

The average high school grade point average is 3.09 for girls and 2.86 for boys. Boys are almost twice as likely as girls to repeat a grade.

Boys are twice as likely to get suspended as girls, and three times as likely to be expelled. Estimates of dropouts vary, but it seems that about one-quarter more boys drop out than girls.

The Center on Education Policy has annually collected results from all 50 states on tests required for accountability under the No Child Left Behind Act. These data show a clear, national trend of males lagging behind females in every state at the elementary, middle, and high school levels.[25]

College:

Among whites, women earn 57 percent of bachelor's degrees and 62 percent of master's degrees. Among blacks, the figures are 66 percent and 72 percent. In federal writing tests, 32 percent of girls are considered "proficient" or better. For boys, the figure is 16 percent.[26]

---

[25] See www.cep-dc.org

[26] See Richard Whitmore, *Why Boys Fail*

The average graduating class at a four-year college is 60 percent women, and women are overtaking men at every level of degree — from associate to Ph.D.[27]

---

[27]   http://www.npr.org/2011/04/04/135114717/boys-educational-achievement-troubles-affects-everyone

Appendix B

The Path of Abundance

The Hope For Your Boys

From an article by Daryl Capuano

Entrepreneurship and Education

I recently met with a young entrepreneur. Graduating from Yale with high honors in math, he had his choice of professional paths and employment opportunities. He chose to start his own company. Since this has become relatively commonplace, I was not surprised.

But, I was surprised by his answer to my question about why he chose this path.

I told him that in my generation there was a brain drain of our best and brightest to investment banking, management consulting, law, and medicine. I asked him if many of his Yale classmates were following these conventional paths to success. "Sure, some, but, that's considered the easy way out, the less interesting thing to do, kind of like you couldn't think of anything else."

This young man was extremely nice and modest. In no way was he trying to put himself above others. But, his answer revealed that the formerly prestigious paths of the high level professions are now considered less prestigious by some than the path of the creators. He was hopeful that he could create work around his passion and, with some hope, get wealthy enough at a young age to avoid the trade-off of the previous generation: decades of ridiculously hard work for wealth later on in time.

This also led me to wonder: what were some factors that helped put this young man in position to create a new venture?

The answer was a mixture of skills, credentials, contacts, and work character.

In terms of his skills, among other areas, he had developed excellent writing abilities. In the new world of work, e-mail and other forms of written communication constitute a large percentage of communication. As a new entrepreneur seeking capital, new clients, business partners and so forth, he sent hundreds of e-mails a week, some quite lengthy, in an effort to get the word out about his company. That was why I agreed to meet with him. I was impressed by the quality of his written presentation.

In addition, his understanding of the numbers required to do well in his business was excellent and his general knowledge of business acquired mostly through reading, since he had no work experience, was outstanding.

Essentially, the three Rs' – reading, writing and arithmetic – were developed at a high level. Sure, he was combining these abilities in a way that would seem foreign to most parents over a certain age but it turns out the fundamentals still matter very much.

In terms of credentials, "Yale" helps open doors to those who might provide capital, become clients or become partners. This is not snobbery. Rather, it reflects the simple truth that in a busy world, we need short hand to decide who to meet. Venture capitalists receive dozens of inquiries every day from would-be entrepreneurs looking for capital. Most VCs will say that the strength of the management team is the number one criteria they focus upon when prospecting a deal. Without an established reputation or work history, young entrepreneurs inspire little confidence and rarely even secure meetings.

Before I continue, I note the following: the skyrocketing costs of private colleges have made the cost-benefit analysis tilt in favor of attending good schools that provide solid economic value over many private schools. In addition, there are numerous jobs and career paths that do not need top schools for entry or success.

With that said, for those seeking outlying success at any early age, top schools are an asset that can be leveraged to pave the path more quickly. During the dawn of the Internet era, I spent a fair amount of time with the leading venture capitalist in the for-profit education space. I vividly remember that most every young entrepreneur that was granted a meeting had attended a brand name college.

As for his contacts, this young entrepreneur had several of his Yale classmates on his new team. New ventures usually have a large challenge in recruiting talent. But, he had a wonderful pool of talent to draw from right in his dormitory. Moreover, the natural network of Yale parents provides an automatic rolodex that is hard to match.

Work character is the largest ingredient that propels success. Indeed, this element of success trumps credentials. And, work character is what creates all those exceptions of people who did not have credentials yet gained outrageous success. The character to persist, work hard, and problem solve are all developed during school. This young entrepreneur clearly had work character in addition to his credentials.

Some of you may have read or heard of <u>The Four Hour Work Week</u> by Tim Ferriss. The quick synopsis: the talented should be able to create a work world that serves their economic interest but allows for a great deal of free time to pursue their passions. Essentially, Ferriss humorously rails against the workaholic craziness of 60 hour work weeks and, in very broad strokes, advocates methods to decrease the amount of time that one works. It is a good read because Ferriss is hilarious and because his general message is extremely hopeful.

Critics point to the unrealistic claims of Ferriss as even the super talented will need to work far more than 4 hours per week. I have a different criticism. Ironically, a guy with a very healthy ego actually fails to note that few people are as smart and energetic as Ferriss (a Princeton grad and a true polymath). For that reason, few could obtain his astonishing success at a young age or any age. With that said, Ferriss does touch on a wonderful point: for those that have the capacity to create their own work world, they can create a wonderful life.

The normal path of graduating college entering the work world, gaining experience in industry and developing skills will remain. But, the talented will have the option to forge their own path at a far earlier age than any previous generation.

The Path of Struggle

The Brave New World of Work For Your Children

From an article published by Daryl Capuano

When unemployment began skyrocketing, I thought of Charles Handy, the British business philosopher who, at one point, ranked second only to Peter Drucker on the list of influential business thinkers. His breakthrough book was The Age of Unreason. This was a great read in the early 1990s. But, as time passed, reading Handy was akin to reading Nostradamus.

Organizations, Handy noted, would shrink to the simplest core of employees possible. Everyone else would become "just-in-time workers", as in employed only when necessary for the good of the core. The core, of course, would be the owners and senior executives.

Essentially, Handy predicted the onslaught of outsourcing, independent contractors, free-lancers, free agents and every other employment structure that has obliterated what, not too long ago, had been the informal notion that once hired, employment would continue into the indefinite future.

Most importantly, Handy predicted that secure jobs would exist for very few. This prediction was not entirely gloomy. Indeed, for some who felt potentially chained to a single company for 40 years, the notion of a job and career shifting world was positively liberating.

The tenets of Handy's predictions are mostly commonplace now. But, many parents are still frozen in time by their career development from twenty years ago. They intellectually understand that the world of work has radically shifted. Many, in fact, experientially understand due to their own job shifting. Yet, many parents are not doing what they can to adequately prepare their children for the daunting employment landscape ahead.

I am an optimist by nature. In this spirit, I clearly see Handy's world unfolding in a way that will leave some small part of the workforce delightfully engaged. Having developed expertise and credentials in areas of market demand, these workers will successfully navigate the new world of work. They will likely have far more interesting, stimulating, and varied careers than their parents. Indeed, the smart, well-educated, hard working students will likely be among those who benefit greatly from this new world of work.

But, my optimism is also tempered by knowing that there will be a major downside for those who do not develop high level skills and credentials.

I think the job seeking landscape of the near future will resemble a nomadic battlefield.

Job seeking warriors will have some combination of credentials, skills, and contacts, to help them battle for preferred jobs, gigs, and projects. The best of the bunch will create their own work.

Your child's future success will depend in no small measure on having developed himself well enough to deal with these new challenges. As a parent, the best thing that you can do for your child's future employment in the daunting new world of work is ensure their abilities are honed at an early age.

The Path of Disaster

The Lost Boys

From an article published by Daryl Capuano

At The Learning Consultants, we have increasingly witnessed an alarming trend of young men, in the 18-24 year old range, who have not fully transitioned from high school into adult life.

Most of them tried some college, either at the community college level or nearby state school. But, for a variety of reasons, college never quite took. Most of them have some type of low pay, non-career building job and most are still living at home.

We call them The Lost Boys.

There are three main points to this article:

(1) to suggest why this trend is occurring
(2) to suggest the need to prevent your teenage boy from becoming one of these Lost Boys and
(3) to suggest the need for action if you have a not-quite adult child in this situation.

Initially, it is helpful to understand how this situation arose. There have always been young adults who did not excel in school and who were not really suited for college. In general, these are the boys who are more physically than scholastically oriented.

During the years of the draft, many of those men would wind up in the army. Unlike those who were eager to get done with their duty, a good number of them would stay in the army. Others, having matured during their army days, would transition into the civilian workforce.

Given our then strong manufacturing sector, many of these men, army or not, could find themselves gainfully employed in solid blue collar jobs. In the summer before I headed off to college, I worked as a shipper on an assembly line. While the guys in the union did not have glamorous jobs, they made reasonably good money, had a steady job, and community. They also could take pride in doing various aspects of the work on the line.

The combination of a volunteer army and well known slide in our manufacturing sector has decimated the standard possibilities for many of these young men.

But, the blue collar work force was not the only place for these action-oriented men to head. Even through the late 20th century, there were solid white collar jobs for those who did not finish college.

There were jobs on Wall St., for those on the floor of the exchange. Stock brokers and other sales jobs did not always require a college degree.

This has changed. Most every large organization requires college degrees for its white collar work force. A college diploma is a simple barrier to entry and a way to sort through thousands of applicants.

What formally was a large separation between those who finished high school and those who did not have a high school degree has shifted to a large separation between those who finished college and those that do not have a college degree.

Indeed, there is no longer a radical difference between someone who finished high school and never attended college and someone who dropped out of college. In both cases, employment prospects are extremely limited.

In terms of the points to consider as a parent, those who become Lost Boys do not emerge suddenly at 18. The tracks of their trail are obvious straight through high school. If they are not interested in school and have grades that will prevent meaningful college choices, then they are on path to wind up on a dead end career track unless you intervene as early as possible. Such intervention could be in many forms such as overseeing their homework, visiting colleges, as well as employing any other inspirational strategy designed to increase motivation.

For those who are already in the situation, massive action is required – NOW.

Those who dug the hole that put them in a rut do not naturally dig themselves out. Intervene as aggressively as possible. Meet with counselors if needed. Do something. Anything. A few years of going nowhere at a pivotal moment in the transformation to adulthood can lead to very challenging circumstances thereafter.

The Path For All Students

The New Economy and the Need for Good Grades

From an article published by Daryl Capuano

To paraphrase Thomas Friedman, author of <u>The World Is Flat</u> who paraphrased Bill Gates:

Twenty years ago, from a purely career-financial perspective, if you had the choice of being a "B" student from Brooklyn or an "A" student from Bombay, you would choose the former because America's economic domination was so thorough that opportunities were abundant for even our average students.

Today, however, many would choose to be the "A" student from Bombay.

Why?

The Internet's power has created an interconnected world that outsources many knowledge based jobs.

In the 80s, many manufacturing economies did not see the challenge of outsourcing until their cities started shutting down.

Many children of those in the manufacturing sector were "educated" with the expectation that they would be working at the local plant when they reached adulthood. Their parents did not put much emphasis on getting a college education. Suffering ensued as there were fewer jobs awaiting unskilled laborers.

There is a similar phenomenon taking place in the lower to mid-range level white collar world.

Those who have jobs that can be done at a fraction of the cost by an English-speaking worker from a different country

(India as the most notable) are losing their jobs at a rapid rate. Perhaps more significantly, those who will be graduating with expectation of abundant entry level white collar jobs awaiting them will be greatly disappointed.

To give but one example, H&R Bloch, the noted tax preparation firm no longer hires thousands of newly graduated Americans with accounting degrees to prepare basic tax returns. Instead, most of the work is done by Indian accountants who work cheaper (and many would say harder and better) than the average new accountant from an average US college.

There is hope. Conceptually challenging work will still be required. And, while there is no doubt that Indians, among others, are quite capable of doing such work, higher end work is far harder to outsource. For example, corporations and high net worth individuals with complicated tax returns still need in-person discussion and time-sensitive management of issues. Those who can perform such work will still be in demand.

Those hired for the more conceptually challenging work will be the "A" students, not necessarily the "B" students and definitely not the "C" students.

The figurative challenge is not as significant as the literal challenge.

Despite the Great Recession, many parents are still in the 1980s-1990s mentality of US world economic domination where jobs were plenty for any student from any college.

They and many of the high school students we meet do not fully understand that getting better grades will have a direct impact on their college choices which, in turn, will have a direct impact on their job prospects.

There are many wonderful opportunities that the new world of work presents. But, those are not prepared with a strong educational background may suffer the same fate as industrial workers in the late 20th century.

About the Author

Daryl Capuano

Through a decade of building The Learning Consultants into the top private tutoring and educational consultancy in Connecticut, Daryl Capuano has developed a deep expertise in motivating students to care about academic success.

Daryl graduated *magna cum laude* and Phi Beta Kappa from Georgetown University, where he graduated number one in his concentration and was named the Outstanding Student in his department. Daryl earned a J.D. from the University of Pennsylvania Law School, where he was named to Who's Who in American Law Students, and an M.G.A. Penn's Fels School. Daryl also earned a prestigious Equal Justice Foundation Fellowship, for which he served at The Brookings Institute, the nation's top think tank. After Penn Law, Daryl was appointed an Assistant District Attorney in Philadelphia where he worked on high profile homicide appeals. Thereafter, Daryl moved to Washington, DC and served the United States as enforcement attorney with the Securities and Exchange Commission and led the investigation into one of the largest financial frauds in history. After serving as an associate with one of the nation's largest law firms, Daryl became Vice-President and General Counsel for Mindgrow, an A&E television-funded new media-education company.

In order to pursue his interest in education and to focus directly on helping students reach their potential, Daryl founded

The Learning Consultants www.learningconsultantsgroup.com. Daryl built the company into a full service academic consultancy with over 25 teachers and educational advisors. The company grew due to its ability create and deliver high quality educational programs that empower students to excel in all academic areas — and in life.

In relation to motivation, Daryl created the Student Mastery Program which provides a holistic framework to help students perform better in school. The Student Mastery Program is unique in its ability to transform the emotional connection students have with their schoolwork and future success and its "Mastery" philosophy which goes beyond helping students succeed in school but provides participants the motivational frameworks to succeed in life.

Recently named to *Who's Who In America,* Daryl has been interviewed in national and local media and is a featured speaker on education issues. In addition to running The Learning Consultants, Daryl is a professor of Constitutional Law, Ethics in International Relations, and several other college courses related to law and government.

Daryl lives in Old Saybrook, Connecticut with his wife and three children, one of whom is a teenage boy.

Made in the USA
Lexington, KY
02 March 2013